# *AGED TO PERFECTION*

## *Prose and Poetry from the Moreno Valley Senior Scribes*

**DADIELTE PRODUCTION**
2014

ISBN: 978-0-9799273-7-9


Published and Distributed by
Dadielte Production
P.O. Box 1266
Moreno Valley, CA 92556-1266


First Printing
Cover design by Sierre' Designs

# *Acknowledgements*

My sincere thanks to all the members of the Moreno Valley Senior Life Story/Creative Writing Class for making this publication possible. It has been my privilege to facilitate this wonderful, talented and inspiring group.

A special thanks to those who helped to put this anthology together - Anne Hendricke Jones for inputting many of the entries, Cathy Fortin-Jenkins who contributed her time and effort towards creating artwork for a cover design, Marcia Hill for photography and Al Turnbull for editing. And thanks to all who entrusted us with your work. Special thanks to Marc Sierre, a talented artist, who generously offered to help put the finishing touch to the project. Last but not least, Jay Jones and the Moreno Valley Senior Center staff who have been very supportive of our efforts. *Anna Christian*

# *Introduction*

When I began facilitating the Moreno Valley Life Story/Creative Writing Class six years ago, we had very few students; three to five who came regularly. From time to time, more came and went. Some have stayed the entire six years. I'm happy to say the class has grown two-fold.

During those six years, we've shared all types of writing- stories from childhood, poignant stories about friends, relatives, significant people who passed through our lives and left indelible impressions; travel adventures, short stories, essays and poems. What better way to showcase our creative endeavors than to put together an anthology featuring a small sample of our efforts; hence, *Aged to Perfection*. The stories in this anthology reflect life lessons, trials and tribulations, challenges, words of encouragement, tributes; stories that made us laugh, some that touched our lives, and some that made us think. It has been an enlightening and enjoyable experience for me.

*Anna Christian*

# CONTENTS BY TITLE

# CONTENTS BY AUTHOR

# A Charismatic Person Walks in a Room and Stops Everything.

## Amelia Garay-Ellis

My friend Bill would be that person. Bill has a smile on his face. Once he enters a room everyone notices that Bill has arrived. He welcomes you with a smile and a compliment, will ask how you are doing; he directs his full attention and acknowledges you, which makes you feel comfortable in seeing him.

Bill is also very intelligent, knows about everything and in his conversations touches most every subject; he also has a sense of humor and very funny in telling jokes, by the end of the night your mouth is sure to be hurting because of the laughter.

He makes you feel loved with a lot of endearment and concern for family members. He loves to reminisce on his past experience and compares the good times to the present.

Bill now lives in Monrovia with his wife, close to Pasadena, Calif. I met Bill through my husband about 27 years ago; we were invited to a Halloween party Bill and his friends were having. I was dressed as a Japanese woman, and as soon as I was introduced to him, I felt comfortable with his conversation and his teasing me about being a Mexican-Japanese was hilarious to me. My stomach was hurting so much from laughing that at one point I had to remove myself from the party to get a breather.

Through the years I noticed that Bill never changed his way of being; I never saw him upset, always upbeat. All his friends also saw him in that way, kind, understanding and a jolly sense of humor. Bill is also a self-taught artist; he is very knowledgeable about art history and in his work shows a lot of imagination and humor. When I would ask him questions about art and showing him my artwork, he would explain techniques he used for his work, and compliment me on my work.

Three years ago Bill was diagnosed with cancer and since then he has been battling a brain tumor. There have been good days, bad days, and one treatment after another, but he was still cheerful and would hide his pain, while coping with the difficult side effects; that's just how his personality was, even reminiscing on past events when he would make me laugh with all his teasing. He was facing his fears quite adequately. I feel that when a person has charisma it never leaves him even when times are hard. The idea of keeping people happy is what matters to him.

Now Bill just sees his close buddies. He will see my husband, but will ask not to bring me; I miss the Bill I knew, who was fun and free spirited that welcomed every one with open arms. I don't care what he looks like, I just want him to know that I miss him and want to have a conversation as we used to about art and share what he knows as to what I know. My husband says that Bill still has a sense of humor and really has not changed in that respect just seeing him not well is what has changed.

Recently we received good news that Bill had been going through a new treatment and it had worked because he is now in remission. Will I see Bill soon? I think so.

# A December to Remember

Cathy Fortin-Jenkins

It was December-a bright frozen day in the early morning and I had awakened to the smell of coffee brewing and bacon frying. The wonderful aromas of breakfast cooking tempted me to arise but the warmth of the two goose-down comforters bade me to stay warm. Then my mother called me and I arose to my unheated upstairs room where only the rising heat of the cook stove in the kitchen gave me a little warmth.

As I hurried to pull on my flannel lined jeans, I remembered that today was to be the day I first used my new white ice skates that I had paid for by myself from my pay for doing chores. The thought of that smooth ice on the pond lured me through a quick splash to my face and a very quick brush of my long hair. I bounced down the stairs in a cheerful mood to greet my mother and to tell her that I wanted to skate with my friends at the pond in Oberlin, a town about two miles away. She asked, "How are you getting there?"

I told her that I was to meet my friends, Dot and Joan and that we were walking to the pond. She said OK and after I helped her clean up the dishes, I was off to meet my friends dressed very warmly with boots, hat, scarf and gloves. We trudged through the foot deep snow and tromped on ice that cracked under our feet. My new white shoe skates with the strings tied together were slung over my shoulder.

When we got to the pond, Nick, a tall slender skater from my church had already swept the snow off the ice with his mother's pilfered broom and was skating backwards around the pond in long legged glides. I was so impressed with his skating. Here I was a novice, only ice skating for the second time in new skates. I had to have my friends help me onto the ice from the tree stump where we donned our skates.

There was a cold wind as I went around the pond for the first time with ankles wobbling but with determination that I would soon skate like Nick as he swooshed past me numerous times to my one time around the pond. I felt very successful and I was soon skating faster than my two experienced friends who were older than me. I did not ever want to stop skating as my gal pals sat on the tree stump for a rest. I skated round and round. I kept an eye on Nick as he went around the pond with that mysterious backward stroke of his blades. I fell a few times, always embarrassed, but always pulling myself up, sometimes with the help of Nick. I loved his attention. I was developing a puppy love crush.

Some of Nick's friends appeared at the fence of the cow pasture and quickly joined Nick on the ice. They speed skated and raced around the pond laughing, hardly out of breath. I tried to stay out of their way by staying to the center of the pond. As I was trying to copy the backward skating, I felt a body slam. I was thrown head first for several yards across that cold, cold ice that was no longer smooth but sliced and diced by the speed skaters. When I came to a stop at the edge of the pond, a lanky fellow that I did not know skated toward me, stopped just short of my feet then pulled me to my feet. This stranger apologized for knocking me down as he grinned slightly with a twinkle in his eye. I thought he was suppressing huge guffaws after seeing me slide across the ice like a hockey puck. I was embarrassed and angry. At the time, I did not know that this young man was to be my husband.

# A Dilemma
## Al Turnbull

One day I cooked my easy homemade chili for lunch. You know, I pour two cans of Dennison's Chili with Beans into a pan; add a small can of tomatoes and a can of beer. While that was heating I fry an onion and some jalapeno chilies to stir in, and then let it boil until it becomes fairly thick. I guess that time the peppers were hotter than normal because my stomach was really upset before I finished a small bowl and I had to drink a second can of beer to sooth my throat.

In the bathroom I took a bottle of Pepto-Bismol from under the sink and shook it vigorously before unscrewing the lid and pouring out a small cupful to relieve my distress. You can visualize my shock when I perceived a pink vapor rising from the now empty bottle! It coalesced into a vague human form about a foot and half high. I immediately saw that I had released a genie.

He was grateful, as you might expect, and he offered to reward me by giving me either an old Cremona violin or a Picasso painting from the master's 'blue period'. I swallowed the comforting chalky liquid while determining which prize I should accept.

Now if I took the violin I could realize an

illustrious career as a virtuoso playing concerts all over the world to admiring audiences. Yes, I could see myself in formal attire in front of the Los Angeles Philharmonic, in the Hollywood Bowl before 10,000 eager listeners, as the orchestra played the long introduction to Beethoven's Violin Concerto. I could also see myself fleeing the stage in panic, for I am a timid person, never comfortable with a crowd looking at me. No, I couldn't accept the Stradivari. I am not cut out for acclaim.

As for the painting: surely a Picasso would be a fine addition to my home. If it wasn't too large, I could hang it above the TV in the family room. Still, I don't know-my renter's insurance would jump to the heavens, and would visitors really believe that they were looking at a real masterwork painted by the most celebrated artist of the twentieth century, on the wall of my $875 a month house in Moreno Valley?

"I'm sorry," I told my vapid visitor. "It is back in the bottle for you. I don't know how to play a violin, and I can't appreciate your painting because I have blue/green color blindness."

My stomach was relieved as I tossed the bottle into the trashcan.

# A Golden Summer Day
Alfred Turnbull

The little boy slept in until nine o'clock. Why not? He didn't have to get up early for anything because it was June and he was on summer vacation. He went downstairs to the kitchen and his mother fixed a bowl of Wheaties for his breakfast. When you are a boy, eight years old, what would be better for breakfast? He finished eating and his mother gave him the only direct order he would have to take that whole, golden June day in 1938.

"Please go brush your teeth and get dressed," she told him.

After a while, he came downstairs and told his mother he was going outside. The backyard was inviting: it was a warm morning in the month of June and he had things to do out there. He inspected, casually – it was quiet at Miss Love's house next door. She would be at work. On the other side, he could hear Mrs. Hartman and Maxine talking. Later, Maxine came out to water the flowers and the little boy went over to the fence to say hello.

The little boy had no one to play with that day in June. His brother and sister were much older, and he wouldn't see any of his cousins unless there was a big family picnic in the park on Saturday. There were neighborhood children, of course, but these were not his friends. They wrestled, rode bikes and played ball. The little boy dismissed such behaviors. He didn't have a bike, and on that day in June he didn't want to have one. He certainly didn't want to fight with anyone, and playing ball wasn't fun. He had a ball, a rubber one that he could bounce on the sidewalk, but that wasn't an interesting thing to do. The ball stayed under his bed upstairs.

The little boy was content to lie on the warm grass. He picked a dandelion and ate the yellow blossom. It didn't taste bad at all. There were also some little plants in the lawn he liked to chew on. His friends, the robins, were busy hunting bugs to eat. The little boy left them alone, just watching, and they didn't mind him, unless he should come too close. He thought that the birds must hear pretty well. He would see them press their heads to the grass and then pick out a bug to eat. The little boy put his head to the ground but could not hear a bug or anything. A pair of blue jays lived in some bushes in the back corner of the yard. They were not friendly. If he came too close, they would chatter at him.

His mother brought him a glass of Kool-Aid and it tasted really good on that warm, free morning.

It was getting warm, so the little boy moved to his swing in the shade of the maple tree. He thought about climbing the tree, but discarded the idea. After all, he could see better from the upstairs windows than up in the tree. After swinging a bit, he went off to hunt for an ant to put on the spider web in the lilac bush. While there, he pulled up a carrot (his mother had planted some vegetables among the flowers), washed it with the hose, and ate it. What is better than a fresh carrot on a morning in June? He lay on his back on the grass for a while and watched the clouds and listened to the bees. Pretty soon his mother called him into the house for lunch. It was wonderful food – tomato soup with crackers to break up in it, and half of a toasted cheese sandwich: a meal that little boys especially like.

After lunch, he went into the living room and practiced his piano lesson for a little while and then went up to his room to check his rock collection. The best rock he had was a hard, shiny, black stone, kind of like glass. It was a piece of obsidian, a treasure, given to him by an aunt who had found it in Yellowstone National Park. Soon it was time to listen to his radio programs, "Orphan Annie" and "Jack Armstrong, the All-American Boy".

Well, this was a vignette about a wonderful, golden day, long ago, a day in June. For this eight-year old boy, life could not be better than this, not ever!

# A Summer Night

## Marcia Hill

Mildred could hear the chimes of the grandfather clock as she alighted from a long warm shower. It was to be a special evening out with her church group. She felt excited about going to her first beach party. She never expected her grandmother to allow her out at night with a group of youngsters to go so far away as Cabrillo Beach. She wrapped herself in a thick lavender towel, and gently squeezed the water from her dark hair, twisting it into a spiral tube that cascaded over her shoulder. The vanity mirror had fogged over during her shower and she reached for the washcloth and used it to dry the mirror so that she could see her reflection. She looked into the glass and gently smiled at the image of a 16-year-old young woman, tall and thin, not extremely pretty, but fresh and pleasing to look at anyway. She hurriedly brushed her teeth and towel dried her wavy hair. If she let it dry naturally, the waves would become loose curls and look nice. She slipped on her undergarments and stepped into her clam diggers, pulled a blue top over her still damp hair jerking it down over the top of her pants, then slipped her narrow feet into white tennis shoes. A quick glance into the mirror reminded her that a little lipstick, light in color, would make her ready to go and join her friends.

Mildred loved the warm summer evening and the noisy conversations that surrounded her. The small church bus rolled down Western Avenue heading south for some thirty miles. The driver was announcing that they had arrived at their destination. As the bus came to a stop, the driver, one of the church chaperones began to lay down the law about expected behavior of the group of about fourteen guys and gals.

"O.K., we're here and I'm gonna take a head count, I got fourteen now and at eleven o'clock, fourteen had better be waitin' at the door of this bus," he said sternly.

His name was Mr. Mitchell, a rather portly man about forty-five years old, already balding on the top of his head. His clothes looked old fashion and so did his glasses. They all knew him and respected the fact that when he spoke he meant business. If they didn't behave, their parents would hear about it. Mildred did not know everyone in the group, but her best friend Shirley stood next to her.

Shirley was looking around the group to see what boys were there. They were carrying the boxes of wieners, buns, chips, and Kool-Aid out to the beachfront where the fire rings were. Mrs. Jones and Mr. Morris were piling some small logs into the pits, stuffing in old newspaper and lighting them

26

to get a fire started. They all got to the pits and started the big roasting event. There was laughter and giggling and now that the fire was high she could get a good look at all in the group.

Mildred asked Shirley, "Did you get the marshmallows off of the front seat?"

She glared at her and rolling her eyes said, "Do you think that 1would have forgotten them? No way, and I didn't forget the coat hangers to put them on either."

This beach has a tremendous amount of broken shells on it as the tide comes in really far. No one took their shoes off because it hurt your feet to walk on the sand. The moon was full and at its brightest, warm breezes flowed past the fire pits sending the smoke back toward the road. Mildred had never felt so free as this moment.

She looked around at the group and her eyes spotted someone that she knew. The young man must have been on the other bus. She was rather shy and did not want to just bust out with a "I didn't know you were here" statement, but he caught her eye and smiled! She got very nervous, her heart started to beat fast and she almost felt faint. He noticed her! Shirley had disappeared in the group and she was more or less by herself.

She began to remember that this guy had stopped in front of her house and held conversations with her grandmother on several occasions. He was quite tall and dark with straight features. His eyes were deep set under heavy eyebrows, a great forehead endowed with a widow's peak formed from his thick dark head of hair. He smiled again and she noticed not only his beautiful white teeth, but he had dimples too! Oh, my goodness.

Mildred decided to reach for her cup of Kool-Aid and as her heart was beating a little fast and her hands a little shaky, of course she spilled some on her blue top. The young man quickly appeared, with napkins in his hands, so close to her she could feel the warmth of his presence.

"Here 1 brought you some napkins. I hope your top won't be stained," he said.

She took them and dabbed at her clothing feeling very embarrassed. "Oh, thank you very much," she said.

Much to her surprise, he then sat down next to her. "My name is Leonard, aren't you Mrs. Waters granddaughter?" he asked.

"Why yes, yes I am. I thought that I recognized you from somewhere," she replied. Feeling less nervous she said, "My name is Mildred."

Sitting on anything at this beach was uncomfortable and Leonard suggested that they walk out to the breakwater that leads to the lighthouse. Mildred agreed and stood up, brushed herself off, and they strolled out across the shell-covered sand dunes. He gave her his hand for support. She felt so protected and enjoyed their closeness.

As they approached the huge rocks that started the breakwater he held her arm and cautioned her to step carefully. The tide had started to come in and the waves were licking the rocks with a bit more force, but the lighthouse was in plain view and so beautiful. Mildred had started to feel like she was in a movie. This handsome young man leading and guiding her steps and then it happened. One large swell of the ocean water washed over the rocky pathway, startling both of them. Mildred's right foot began to slide and she cried out in fear.

"Oh, my god, that was close and 1 don't swim!" she uttered with a trembling voice. "We had better go back, don't you think?"

Leonard responded with self-confidence, "Don't be frightened. I wouldn't let anything happened to you, but we can go back."

They carefully walked back to the sandy shore and then she looked at him and their eyes met and in a moment he kissed her on the lips. A warm and loving kiss that said without words, 'I think that I love you.' Mildred kept her eyes closed even after their embrace was over. She thought to herself, this is the first time that I have been kissed. How beautiful the setting and how magical it was. A summer night to never be forgotten.

# A Tree

Mona Lisa Stallworth

If I came back to earth, I would return as a tree. It would not matter which species: be it a fruit or nut bearing tree that provides food or a flower blossoming tree that makes the air smell wonderful and is a delight to the eyes. It would not matter if they cut me down and turn me into paper for use by brilliant writers, scientists or just kids or maybe I could be made into lumber to build beautiful homes and buildings. No, it really would not matter!

As a tree I could live to be thousands of years old- well, unless I am planted in the city; then my life expectancy would be about 8 years. But that would be fine, too, because even during this short life span I would be keeping the air supply clean. I alone could absorb as much carbon in a year as a car produces while driving 26,000 miles. That means over the course of my lifetime I could absorb one ton of carbon dioxide.

Did you know a tree can produce 260 pounds of oxygen a year? And if someone planted another tree near me the two of us mature trees could supply enough oxygen to support a family of four. As a mature tree I can remove almost 70 times more pollution than a newly planted tree. And as a healthy mature tree I can be worth as much as $10,000- not bad for an old tree.

Yea, and do not judge what I can do by my height. I could grow to be 328 feet tall but even if I only grew 100 feet tall and had a diameter of 16 inches I could produce enough paper and wood to supply one person's needs for these products for a whole year!

That's not all trees can do for mankind. Properly placed trees can reduce air condition needs by 30%. Some really smart people have said that the net cooling effect of a young healthy tree is equivalent to having 10 room size air conditions operating 20 hours a day, amazing! Trees can also reduce heating costs in the winter- time.

You want to hear some more things I could do as a tree? Well, here goes; as a tree I would keep the noise level down, prevent soil erosion and improve water quality. Also a large tree can lift up to 100 gallons of water out of the ground and discharge it into the air!

Now I could go on and on about how I beautify the landscape, add value to property, provide shelter for wildlife and birds of all type. But I think you get the picture as to the many reasons why I would chose to come back as tree.

But can I tell you a secret? Would you like to know my personal all-time reason for wanting to return as a tree?

It's the children! Yes, the kids!! I would love to hear the sound of their laughter as they use me as home base for their game of hide and seek or run around me while playing tag. I would love to be the center of their playtime. They could climb me and sit on one of my branches and pretend all sorts of things. Someone could build a tree house for them and I could have their company day and night. The thought of them tying a rope around my branches to make a swing brings joy to my heart. And my ability to provide them with a healthy snack of fruits or nuts would just be icing on the cake. That would be a life worth living. So a tree I would be!

# *Aging Ain't For Sissies*
James Kraft

This 87 year old is happy to accept any old age perks that come my way, including people opening doors for me, letting me ahead of them in lines, unloading my shopping cart, senior discounts, and free hugs.  I think some people show kindness to me because I may remind them of past grandparents.  Except for the senior discounts and hugs, I don't always accept perks.  I feel useful if I can do my own thing.  Also, I can be slightly eccentric without too much concern by others.

Major aging drawbacks for me are a sense of proper balance.  I "list" when I walk.  My doctors have performed numerous tests, scans, imaging, and drug substitutions but to no avail.  Unbalance is a complicated body function.  I have to be careful stepping up and down curbs and getting out of bed slowly to avoid dizziness.

At old age, falls can be disastrous.  Over the past several months, I have had two major falls.  One was caused by our over-exuberant house pet; a sixty-pound, docile pit bull who jumped on me from behind when I entered our home.  I fell forward to the floor which resulted in five fractured ribs.  I can't remember experiencing anything more painful and debilitating. I was helpless. My recovery was based on pain pills and inactivity. My resident older daughter was my caregiver. She had to help me up and sit me down. I had to use a walker to get to the bathroom and needed help to get my pants down. I recovered.

My next fall was exiting the bathtub shower when I braced myself relying on a grab handle fastened to the shower wall. It pulled loose and down I went. Going down, I pulled loose the shower curtain and the shower rod, falling half out of the tub. My feet were hanging over the edge of the tub and my rear end was on the floor. The shower water was running and I am helpless half in and out of the tub, wrapped in a shower curtain. It's early AM and the family is still asleep so my calls for help go unanswered. If I am sitting on the floor, I cannot directly get up without assistance. I can crawl to some room structure to brace myself and pull myself up. I survived, no broken bones but bruised soft flesh.

I started using a cane for walking support after my two major fall-down episodes. I use it around the house, shopping, going to and from my auto, and going upstairs to my room. I did not use the cane at my hospital job. I have a growing physical problem with my volunteer job at Riverside County Regional Medical Center (RCRMC). My present assignment is a Mon-Wed-Fri, 4 ½ hour stint from 6:30 AM to 11:00 AM. I am at my physical limit.

I feel I am getting close to seeing the white light at the end of the tunnel as far as my present job is concerned. It was (is) getting scary for me to continue my job area of responsibility, which involves walking various distances between medical units. I feel I will just have to stop. I feel my co-workers have not detected my physical disabilities.

I have a wonderful volunteer job at Riverside County Regional Medical Center in Moreno Valley. I wear my uniform with my volunteer badge. It makes me feel important. I give walk-in cancer patients fruit juice, cookies, and engage willing patients in small talk and do non-medical tasks for the clinic RNs. I try to hide my unsteady gait when my shift is over and I am leaving home. When I get home, I lay down to take a nap. If I don't take at least a two-hour nap, I feel I will fall over. I have become a half-day man. I talked to my daughter about my condition.

She said, "Why don't you take your cane to the hospital job?"

I told her I was vain and I didn't want people to think I was handicapped, and I never saw any medical personnel using a walking assist.

She said, "You are stupid. Use your cane at the hospital before you fall down."

I took my cane to work with me. I overcame a major, mental hurdle. People have their own problems and don't have time to be concerned about you. Just who do you think you are? Using the cane does help me but the major problem is still there. I told my sister about my vanity and what I thought people would think.

She said, "I have a good insert for your story. It is from a Scottish poem which goes, 'Oh, what a tangled web we weave when first we practice to deceive'."

Today, I have an appointment with my primary physician, the subject of which is "fatigue and tiredness". I have my medication list all typed up for her to review. I think she will set me up for blood work. I expect her to have a list of possible causes for my condition and the last item will be "he is 87".

# Aneta Street

Linda Moore

We moved into our house when I was two years old. It was a three bedroom, 11/2 bath home with an apple tree in the backyard and tomato bushes lining both sides of the house with their splendid colors. The house was brand new and was painted a light shade of pink. I believe it was around 1000 square feet. To me, it was huge! There were about five blocks of similar houses in our tract, all on the right side of Centinela Boulevard. Nearby was Lopez Ranch, where you could pick fruits and vegetables at your leisure and if you wanted, you could walk right down to the beach. It wasn't far.

The neighborhood school, Playa del Rey Elementary School was two blocks away. It was also brand new. Before you got to the school, you had to pass right by Playa del Rey Market where most of us stopped to get treats, like five cent candy, or potato chips and if we had more money, we could buy a Coke or a Twinkie. Whatever the popular snack was, you could find it at Playa del Rey Market for sure. Near the market was dry cleaners where my parents brought their fancy clothes that couldn't be washed and dried in the standard old washer and dryer.

Aneta Street was also right down the street from Hughes Airport and around the corner from the Centinela Bowl, Mar Vista Theater and many types of restaurants. Us kids loved to get on our bicycles and ride down to the bowling alley or just watch the airplanes take off from the runway. If we were really bored, we walked through the fields and maybe just saw some ripe strawberries or some nice squash before it was picked for market.

One time I remember walking through the fields on a blistery summer day when I heard a gun shot as loud as could be exactly where I was standing. Well, not for long. I jetted across that field so fast I thought my legs would take off without my body. I was that scared! I ran and ran. Finally, I made it home and I was in one piece, but a wreck! I waited at least a week before I tried that again. Apparently, a convict had run away from the nearby prison and nobody knew it right away. That is, until I called 9-1-1. Before you knew it, there were row upon row of police cars right on my block waiting to catch this guy! Things like that happened fairly regularly. The good news was, the bad guys were almost always caught.

Being near a ranch, made it easy prey for criminals to hide. Our street was short. It dead-ended three houses away from where I lived. The ranch had row upon row of various fruits and vegetables...and when that ended there was row

38

upon row of Eucalyptus and other local trees as well. Aneta Street was probably typical of most middle class streets in America in the 50's. There were many youngsters in my little area. A few houses had neighborhood pools in their backyard. So, most of the time we congregated in these.

# Be Your Own Masterpiece

Anna Chase

A quote by an unknown author states: "Why compare yourself with others? No one in the entire world can do a better job of being you than you."

Comparing ourselves to others is something we all do, or have done at some time in our life.

When we hear other people talking about things like a recent job promotion, a vacation to some exotic place, or other exciting events or accomplishments, we may find ourselves comparing our lives to theirs. Even though we may be happy for their good fortune, the danger occurs when we see what is present in their life as something that is lacking in ours.

If you think about it, we hardly ever compare ourselves with someone who is less fortunate and then consider ourselves blessed. More often, we compare ourselves with others who we perceive as being smarter, more productive or better in some way than us.

It may help to remember that someone else may be looking at you in the same way and wishing their life was more like yours.  It seems to be true, like the old saying goes, that "the grass is always greener on the other side."

When we fall into the trap of trying to be more like someone we admire, or dare I say envy, perhaps we should focus instead on our positive attributes and accomplishments.  Every day we are learning, growing, and becoming more of who we are meant to be based on the decisions we made yesterday.  We are in a constant state of expansion within ourselves.

So, when you catch yourself making a comparison to someone else, stop and think about what you are doing today that you couldn't do a year ago.  Ask yourself if you have done anything new or in any way moved in a new direction to better your life or your relationships?  Have you done anything that you never thought you could do?  Or, have you let go of a negative behavior and replaced it with a positive one? These are the things that count.  Comparing yourself to someone else will cause you to lose focus on what is important to your own growth.

Ultimately, the most important comparison we can make is the one from our past self to our present, and hopefully better self.

Michelangelo said, "Every block of stone has a statue inside it and it is the task of the sculptor to discover it."

So, be your own sculptor and discover the one-of-a-kind masterpiece that is uniquely you.

# *Daydreamer*
Anna Chase

I can travel to Rome and see the Dome
Stop off in Paris on the way home.
I don't need a passport, a suitcase or cash
Just a head full of dreams and some time to pass
I can ride a camel or swim with a mammal
Go anywhere, do whatever I dare.
Some call me lazy but what do I care
I can kiss Brad Pitt without leaving my chair.

# Brother Allen

### Anna Christian

When Brother Allen first appeared at Bible Study, all the single women were drooling at the mouth. Not because he was particularly handsome, but because he was tall, over 6 ft., muscular, broad shoulders with a trim frame as if he'd spent years working out, his voice deep like Barry White, and his smile, daunting. His complexion was the color of rich dark chocolate; he wore his hair clipped short and the one gold tooth stood out among the white ones giving him the appearance of a hustler, a gigolo. He was studying for the ministry so he said, as he quickly became involved in the discussion.

We continued our bible study lesson though some of us found it difficult to concentrate with him sitting nearby. At the end of the hour, when the pastor asked him to pray, he prayed like he'd been praying since he'd been born. His prayer was so powerful I had to peek to get a look at his face and wonder what kinds of sins he'd committed. The brother was working it. When he was done, we females gathered around him like hungry chickens in a hen house each vying for his attention.

The very next Sunday there was Brother Allen sitting up in the pulpit on the front row with the other ministers. After service, everyone went over to the Washington's house for the annual Christmas party. We ate a lot, exchanged presents, played games, and generally had a good time relating to each other in a different setting.

I don't think I was the only single female aware of his presence.  Trying not to be too obvious, I watched him. He was friendly, even a little flirty as he spoke to as many of us as he could, asking questions and telling us about himself. He was a contractor and had built his house in Perris surrounded by acres of land. He offered to help us ladies with whatever we needed. "Any time you ladies need anything done, don't hesitate to call me. I'm at your service," he said, his deep voice sending chills up and down my spine. "In return all I ask is for a good home-cooked meal. You know us bachelors," he chuckled. "We don't take good care of ourselves." I could see he was a real gentleman.

A few weeks later, he came over to my house and mowed my backyard. Can't remember how that came about. I'm not a cook; I cook for myself, but I'm not a gourmet or one who likes to cook for others. After he'd mowed I was amazed at how good my backyard looked.  Until he took to it with the lawnmower, my backyard was a field of weeds.

44

He even washed the machine off when he was done. I thanked him and promised I'd cook him a scrumptious meal next time. Well, that was that. There was no next time. I guess I wasn't his type. I soon realized he wasn't mine either.

Then I began noticing he and Sister Davis slipping out together or coming late into church service together. It was interesting to watch them, knowing they thought they were hiding their relationship from the rest of us. I wasn't in on the gossip, but I heard rumors. Whenever they were together, Sister Davis was all smiles. He would grin sheepishly.

But Whoosh! Just like that, Brother Allen disappeared. We never saw him again. I learned later that he had been wooing several ladies in the church before settling on Sister Davis. Don't know what happened between them. What I do know is that he's gone. She's still here and carrying no tales.

# Bulls in My Life

### Rene Walter Madayski

Mokre, a beautiful little village in the county of Pszczyna, where in the 1860's the last free roaming bison was shot by its count, was my home. Our mansion, on a large agricultural estate in which I, the youngest of four was borne, had the service entrance in the back facing a courtyard of about a dozen 15 foot wide cement steps leading to the business office and adjacent kitchen, ice and baking room. We children as well as those of the families employed permanently by the estate, like the blacksmith, saddle maker, chauffer, wagon maker etc. were using the steps as a gallery for an amusing spectacle. While the mansion had all utilities, the cottages lining the first court had no running water; it had to be fetched from a pump in the middle of the court. The horse and cow stables lined the adjacent second court. Milking was done by hand, and after it the cows were led to pasture, weather permitting. Their manure was loaded on a flat sled pulled by the main bull from the aisles to the manure heap in front of the stables. Pan Jakubovsky, the head milker in charge of the cow stable, led the bull with a 3-foot-Iong stick clamped to a ring in the nose of the bull. After the manure was removed from the stable the bull was let loose for a good part of an hour to roam in both courts with the gate of the second court leading to the street, closed. It was a game of courage for the mostly young wives of the smith, tractor driver, saddle maker and our chauffer, whose cottages lined the first court, to fetch water from the well when the bull was roaming freely in both courts. A number of times he came charging towards the lady attracted by the swinging of the pump handle and the swaying of their skirts. We spectators had a good laugh or applause when the woman dropped the pail and sometimes their pantoffels to seek safety in their homes or at our steps. Once a lady fled up the steps and the bull charged her. I, sitting on one of the lower steps, fled in horror to the top. The bull fortunately stopped at the lowest step. For days afterwards I had nightmares of the bull charging me with gusto and I, trying to run up the steps, was running in place not being able to leave the first step. When the beast lowered his head to spear me with his sawed off horns, I would wake up, drenched and crying. About two decades later a somewhat similar encounter became almost near reality.

As a graduate student at the University of Michigan, I was asked by a colleague if I wanted to accompany him on a plant collection trip through Mexico, since I spoke some Spanish. Since Monardas, plants of my interest also grew down there, this would be a splendid opportunity for observation and some fieldwork, I agreed to accompany him on condition that we also would find time to visit museums, archeological sites, colonial structures and for me Sunday services.

Bill worked on ragweeds, the genus Ambrosia, a major hay fever culprit and had funding from N.l.H. for this trip. He just did not want to drive alone. Thus in a university station wagon, loaded with plant presses, film and camping gear we took off. We had excellent results collecting already in the southern states, and were also dumbfounded by the "Whites only" signs at gas station toilets. We were delayed at Laredo for over a day, because the Mexican official wanted to be paid, but our budget simply did not allow for bribes, and crossed a day later at Piedras Negras. We now faced an unexpected desert spring flood, later got lost in Vera Cruz and participated in the 100-year celebration of the ouster of La Legion Etrangere in Puebla in 1862. We had no teaching assignment during the summer months and thus ample time to take part in historical celebrations.

At the end of our trip, on the way back from Jalisco, in the upland meadows of Durango, on a logging road in an Indian reservation, the nightmare of my youth almost came true. There was a rolling meadow studded with pine trees and on occasional manure spots were thistles and one species of my
48

mountain Monardas. The area was fenced in with six strands of barbed wire nailed to trees stems or wooden posts. We halted close to a tree where the wires were nailed to and had a branch on which one could swing into the meadow, about four feet above the upper wire. I swung over and went ever further into the meadow, bent over looking intently for my Monarda austromontana flower heads for mature seeds to collect.

Suddenly I had an ominous feeling of being watched. In still bent position, I looked ahead and to my horror saw a herd of bulls, one only 30 or so yards away. He was not the fat Holstein bull of my youth with sawed off horns, but a lean, muscular fighting bull with shiny horns like those bred for the arenas. He looked at me intently. In a still bent position, I went backwards, step by step. I dropped everything; an inner voice told me, "If you flail your arms and run, he will charge you." Through my mind flashed the frescos of the Mycenaean bull dancers of ancient Crete; the trampled bodies of boys during the bull run of Pamplona, Spain; or a gored torero during a torrida in some Hispanic town. Would my legs stop moving as in my nightmares?

I moved back slowly in a zigzag fashion from tree to tree and saw that the bull followed slowly. When I thought that I could reach the fence, I turned and ran. I heard the bull charge. I reached

49

the fence, jumped up the tree, grabbed the branch and swung over. However my left leg hit the wire and a barb tore a delta wound into it. I limped to the nearby car, and poured a generous portion of hydrogen peroxide from our medical kit over the now bleeding triangular hole. I calmed myself down, assuring myself that the Tetanus shot received before leaving Michigan would prevent any disease. The bull did not crash into the tree or wire. From Michigan we sent a set of collected herbarium sheets to the Mexican National Herbarium as a courtesy since these were their plants and we were not charged for collecting them. As a token of my appreciation I published in1969: EI Gernero Monarda en Mexico, in the Boletin de la Sociedad Botanica de Mexico, 30: 31-71. This excursion into the interior of the country was my first, and the basis for my lasting enthusiasm for its people and the numerous archeological sites of its diverse pre-colonial Mesoamerican high cultures spanning about 3000 years. Reminiscing, I feel like shouting con gusto, " Viva Mexico".

# *Color*
## Phillip Sanchez

I had to break away from the norm this day. Lately my life has become too cluttered with people and things pulling me back and forth like a rubber band. Along with about 30 other fisherman, I'm out in the Mighty Pacific Ocean this day on the swift fishing boat, called the "San Diego" out of the Sea Forth Sport Fishing Landing in San Diego; three-fourths day boat.

Clear beautiful day, can see for miles, our boat swiftly moving through the sea swells, the sound of sea water slightly rushing on either side of our boat. Boat gently rocking as it penetrates the ocean surface. North wind touches my face. The scent of clean salt water permeates the air. We've left the past, no thoughts of who we are or what we do for a living.

No connecting with what we left behind, on shore and land, just your boat, you, fellow fishermen and the Magnificent Pacific Ocean.

All of a sudden we all hear an anxious fisherman yell, "hook up" which is our signal that he caught a first catch for the boat off of a trolling line. There is a school of fish rushing by our boat. We all quickly bait our lines and cast out searching for our first catch, adrenaline racing through our bodies and exciting our lives and existence.

Then, out of a long waiting moment I feel the hit of my fish, whoa, what power! What force! It pulls my line. I can hear the line being pulled out by this mighty force. I reel and reel fast, keeping my line taut, never letting up. But, this fish is strong and mighty; it pulls out more and more of my line; I quickly reel in again and again, back and forth we go, this battle goes on and on. "This must be a monster," I'm thinking to myself. Then, after almost seven minutes, I finally yell "color" which means that I have brought my fish to the surface and next to our boat. A crew hand runs to me responding to my "color" calling. He gaffs the fish and brings him up on the boat deck. What a rush! What a feeling of euphoria, my first catch!

Such was this day that I needed oh, so much. Such a Great Feeling enjoying God's Great Gift and three good-size Yellow Fin Tuna.

# Commencement 2013

C.V. Schweitzer

The applause slowly subsided as Doctor Mayberry approached the microphone. "Ladies and gentlemen, mothers and fathers and the many friends and relatives who have come here today to witness the passage of another milestone in these young people's lives: Welcome."

"Most of you know me, but to those who don't, I am Doctor John Mayberry, Principal of this great learning institution. On behalf of the faculty of Lincoln High School I want to welcome you to the graduation ceremonies of Class 2013.

The horrible incident that occurred on Monday, the 3rd of March 2013 has in some way or other affected everyone gathered here today. For two of our students, it has unfortunately changed their lives forever. As you know, Albert Cox is in police custody."

A hush of sadness fell upon the crowd awaiting the next name to pass his lips. Suddenly the air exploded into thundering applause and cheering as a young woman in a wheel chair was pushed on to the stage.

When the standing ovation finally subsided, Doctor Mayberry continued; "Two weeks ago

Susan Hamath had a relapse, and her recovery and her ability to join us today had been in doubt. That was until last Tuesday when I received a call from Doctor Goldman with a very unusual request. He told me what he was purposing would help Susan in her recovery. Well, after what she had done for this school, who could say no? But then I found out what he was asking would affect two of our finest and brightest students."

Doctor Mayberry turned to the row of teachers and students seated behind him, "Alison, will you please stand."

As the young woman came to her feet Doctor Mayberry introduced her, "Ladies and gentlemen it gives me great pleasure to introduce Lincoln High School's 2013 Senior Class Valedictorian, with a grade point average of 4.0: Miss Alison Bromfield."

When the applause subsided he continued. "Philip, please stand. Ladies and gentlemen it gives me great pleasure to introduce your Lincoln High School's 2013 Senior Class Salutatorian with a grade point average of 3.9: Mr. Philip Archer."

Turning back to the audience he looked out into the front row,

"Mr. and Mrs. Bromfield and Mr. and Mrs. Archer you have raised two remarkable young people. When Alison and Philip heard that Susan's speaking to you would help her in her healing they wholeheartedly agreed to yield her their time."

As the applause died away and the assembly settled back in their seats, Doctor Mayberry adjusted the microphone and turned to Susan and whispered, "The stage is yours."

Susan Hamath cleared her throat as the young lady who had pushed her out on to the stage locked the brakes on her wheelchair. Turning her head towards Alison and Philip she mouthed, 'Thank you" then turned back to the crowd.

"Most of you know I'm a transfer student. I joined the class of 2013 on the 3rd of January. In less than a week my presence in the hallways was heralded by 'Sooie Pig!' which one would expect if one was attending the University of Arkansas, but alas that was not the case. Such recognition of my presence was not new to me or unexpected. At Central High it was 'Hamath the Hippo'"

Susan took a deep breath and let it out slowly, "Well as to what happened that fateful Monday morning, both Albert and I had made our way through the usual harassing calls to Mr. Water's 8 o'clock History class. We were all settling into our respective seats when one of the boys, I won't say who, called Albert a 'four eyed homo'."

As a gasp came from the crowd Susan continued. "Oh, that's one of the nicer things. I couldn't and wouldn't repeat some of the other ones. I guess Albert finally just snapped. I remember the gun and hearing the sound.

"Susan took another deep breath, "That was it until I awoke up two days later to the worried faces of my parents with the new title of Heroine. The flood of get-well cards and flowers engulfed my room. And the accolades on TV and the Governor's award were overwhelming. When I returned to school, suddenly, I found myself one of the in-crowd. They were fighting over who would push my wheelchair. I had an entourage everywhere I went."

Susan glanced over her shoulder at the young woman who had pushed her out on the stage. "Cindy told me they had a lottery to see who would push me out today.

"As you already know I had a relapse two weeks ago. It wasn't physical. My mind just couldn't take it anymore. I couldn't understand how my one act could change my status in my classmates' eyes from pariah to heroine. I could rationalize all the words that were used to reflect my weight, let's face I'm fat. And when it comes to my looks according to all the young women's magazines you read, I'm homely. But Heroine! I don't know how many times I ask God,"

Susan made a gritting grinning face. "Oh sorry about that I forgot public funded building. I ask Him why he let me live like this." She pointed at the wheelchair. Susan paused then reflected.

"As I lay there in the hospital I began to

56

analyze why and how does someone become a bully? Bullying is not passed down genetically. Well, the scientific community hasn't been able to isolate a bullying gene so far. And I can't remembering any school curriculums offering: Bullying 101."

Susan tilted her head upward with a questioning look on her face. "So if a baby's brain is a clean slate when it is born, just where do they learn these bullying traits? Scientists say we are the product of our environment. Some even suggest that learning begins in the womb. Maybe the parents of the six boys that Albert had on his hit list could help us with the answer."

"You know the saddest part of this story is that of a young man who was in the contention for class Valedictorian. A young man who had already received four college acceptance letters including one from West Point."

Susan paused then slowly shook her head. "With Albert's potential who knows what he might have contributed to our society? Now it's all gone and for what, I ask you ladies and Gentleman, and for what?"

"Several days ago the answer to my question came to me in a dream. A voice told me it was to make this speech."

"You see, of all the words that I've ever been called, Heroine was the most painful." Susan gestured with her right index finger. "Believe it or not that one word was the reason for my relapse. Doctor Goldman made me understand that it was my upbringing that wouldn't allow my mind to accept the honors and accolades for what I had done."

When I was a little girl my grandfather listened to a radio commentator named Paul Harvey. He became famous for broadcasting, 'The News of the Day', and then he would tell 'the rest of the story'. In the tradition of Paul Harvey now it's time for the rest of my story."

Susan took a deep breath and let it out slowly. "You see on that fateful morning I too, like Albert, had been pushed to the brink. Her voice quivered as she continued. When I saw the gun I didn't stand up to shield my fellow classmates. I stood up to be first."

# *Culture Shock*

## Phillip Sanchez

According to Wikipedia, the free encyclopedia: Culture Shock is a term used to describe the anxiety and feelings (of surprise, disorientation, confusion, etc.) felt when people have to operate within an entirely different cultural or social environment, such as a foreign country.

Now, I'm going to take you back in time, many, many years ago to when a little five year-old left the safety and comfort of home for his first day of formal schooling in the public school system.

Where: Central Los Angeles

Time: 1952

Situation: First day in elementary school

Who was it? Yes as you probably figured out it was yours truly.

Yes, there I was, a small, shy, unknowing innocent child attending my first day in school in kindergarten. I was pretty excited and to some extent, fearful.

That was the scene for what was going to be My First...Culture Shock!

It was the first hour of the first day. Each student was asked to go to the blackboard and write, then, say their name. All the students before me went up and wrote, then stated their names. Then, came my turn.

But wait, wait, I forgot to tell you a little bit more about me. My parents raised me <u>speaking only Spanish</u>. English was only introduced when I was about four-years-old. So, I spoke and understood mostly Spanish with a slight understanding of English.

Now: To continue with my story. First hour of first day in kindergarten,

One by one each student went up and wrote their name, then spoke their name: John Smith, Jane Warner, etc. Finally, it was my turn.

I walked slowly to the board, took the chalk and wrote my first name:

F E L I P E and started on the S of my last name, Sanchez. No sooner had I finished writing my first name Felipe and started the S in Sanchez, the teacher stood up and yelled at me in a mean hateful voice in front of the whole class.

"No, No, No! That is not your name"

I was in Shock, what did I do? I put my head down, feeling ashamed, but I still managed to say, "My name is Felipe Sanchez" in a soft humbled voice.

She yelled, "No, it is not!"

She stopped everything, rushed to me and grabbed my hand and escorted me out of the classroom to the Principle's office. So, there I am, my first hour of my first day of class having committed my first crime.

Once in the Principle's office I waited, waited, and waited. Finally, my parents showed up. My parents were very humble, religious and respectful, especially respectful of authority figures. They were very humiliated and embarrassed and insulted being informed that they should not be speaking any, I mean, any Spanish to me.

As you can see, it was a day I will never, ever forget. So what were the effects of my first Culture Shock? From that day forward, my parents spoke no more Spanish to me. The result: on the upside – I did improve my English speaking skills that did help complete my college education and get a good job. But, on the downside – I lost my language and my culture which was really devastating. So, that was my first encounter with Culture Shock.

Now, fortunately our nation has grown up a bit, thank God. Our country now somewhat embraces Cultural Diversity where differences are cherished and encouraged; Thereby forcing us to take a brand new look at personal prejudices and narrow-mindedness; opening our hearts to each other.  Just look around at our Club Membership.   It is great – we are a universal, culturally diverse club!  So, that is my story of my encounter with Cultural Shock.

I'll close by saying I sincerely hope that you will never, ever have to experience or endure the demon, the prejudice of Culture Shock.

# *Doren*
## Edith Nevins

Doren is a Great Dane that came into the Nevins' household as a puppy. At that time, I had five boys and we were living in a large single house in Cleveland, Ohio with a large front porch and a decent size backyard. The ages of my sons were 5-13.

Doren was shipped to our house from Brooklyn, New York by Lewellyn McFarlane, godfather of my oldest son, Albert. My husband and I told the boys that it was their duty to take care of the puppy because it was their gift.

The boys took turns feeding and walking the puppy up and down the street. As Doren became larger, two boys together had to walk him around the neighborhood and in the local parks. The neighborhood children began to view the Nevins boys as untouchable because no one wanted that large Great Dane to jump on them-his bark was worst than his bite. Doren came early in the spring by airplane and many afternoons, boys and dog could be found sitting on the front porch playing together. Adults and children chose to walk in the street instead of walking in front of my house. As he grew larger, he had a good appetite and the children had to clean up behind him-part of dog ownership.

Doren and the five sons lived together for 17 years. After the last son left home, he was alone and did not leave the porch. He died in the basement and I called two sons to come and take the body away. It was 17 years of family activities in the Nevins' household.

# Finding Mr. Right

*Anna Chase*

It's early Saturday morning and Dee just finished her Pilates. Keeping fit and trim gets harder and harder as she nears her 50$^{th}$ birthday, but those Botox treatments are nothing short of miraculous. Dee walks around her stylish downtown loft, cooling down, and catches her reflection in the new art deco mirror. She looks pretty good and her recently redecorated apartment looks great. She even has a job she loves. Dee finally has everything just the way she wants it; everything, that is, except someone to share it with.

It would be nice, Dee thought, to have someone to do things with, like go to movies, dinners, plays, and on trips. Not that she did much of these things in her last relationship, which ended after just two years, one of which was spent cohabitating – in her apartment. She met Rick in a bar where she was taking swing dance lessons. Their so-called "dating" was mostly centered around dinner in front of the TV watching Monday Night Football or auto racing. On rare occasions they might spend a weekend playing the slots at a local casino with dinner at a cheap buffet.

Dee's sister kept telling her she should check out some online dating sites like their friend Jess did. Even though it took almost a year of emailing, phone calls and coffee dates, Jess finally met someone she really liked and thinks she may have found her soul mate.

Dee always thought on-line dating sites were for the young, but taking her sister's advice she logged on to the "Catch-a-Fish" website and started looking at pictures and reading profiles. There were smart looking grey haired men, even a few with moustaches – she always did like a good moustache; and some even said they were seeking a lasting relationship with women in her age group. Did she dare pursue it further?

Looking back on past relationships, Dee realized she hadn't done so well on her own. After all, I trust my computer with so many other things, she thought, like paying my bills, shopping, picking out books and movies; even planning trips. Why not let it help me find someone to share my life with? Still feeling a little reluctant, she decided to think about it while working on her tan down at the pool. Maybe she'd start tomorrow.

She took the elevator down to the pool level and, just as she stepped out, a very attractive man winked at her and smiled as he entered the elevator going up. Dee remembered hearing that someone had recently moved into the penthouse suite and she wondered if this was the guy. At the same time she was wondering where she had seen him before. He looked so familiar. Then it dawned on her. Could it be? Was he one of the men she recently admired online? She decided to forget her tan, rushed back up to her apartment and logged on to the "Catch-a-Fish" website. She scrolled quickly through her list of favorites and sure enough, there he was -- Bob W. Could this really be the same guy? It sure looked like him, but how could she be certain? I know, she thought, and off she went to check the apartment directory. Dee did a double take and almost laughed out loud when she saw the name on the directory – Robert Wright. Dee shook her head and stifled another laugh. I can't wait to tell my sister. Mr. Right just moved in upstairs!

# Forever Prop Boy
Jim Kraft

I have always been obsessed with airplanes and
flying, then and now. During the 1940s I was a
sixteen-year-old high school student who spent
weekends at a small airport located at Elmhurst,
Illinois, a suburb of Chicago. I was an airport
groupie who could never absorb enough flying
atmosphere. As I became more familiar with the
airplane mechanics and airport personnel, I would
pester them with questions and do errands for them.
This airport hosted a small flying school that
survived on weekend income derived from students
receiving flying lessons. The school's livelihood
depended on three J3 Piper Cub trainers; a popular
two-piece, easy-to-fly, no frills basic airplane.

In the early 1940s these J3 Cubs were priced at
$999 FAF (fly away at factory) from Lock Haven,
Pa. Today this airplane is a classic, priced in the
tens of thousands. The J3 Cub's simplicity and
popularity compares to the Ford Model T. This
airplane is no longer in production. It is estimated
20,000 were built during its time in the sun. It was
also used by the U.S. military in World War II. It
was the perfect trainer for fledging pilots. It was
very docile and forgiving. Cruising speed was 75
MPH. It came with a 65 HP engine and had a

68

twelve-gallon fuel tank. Range was about 220 miles. Okay, enough about the hardware.

Maximum effort was expended to make sure these three trainers were flyable on weekends. The flight school hired off-duty airline pilots as weekend flight instructors. I was offered a weekend job to help refuel the trainers when they returned to the field after their student lessons. After I became more familiar with the airplanes, I was taught how to manually spin the propeller to start the engine. The trainers had no self-starter; this had to be done by hand. This procedure had to be followed religiously.

The student sat in the back and the instructor sat in the front (tandem seating). The airplane was positioned to avoid any ill effects due to forthcoming propeller blast after the engine started. Removable wheel chocks were positioned in front of each wheel for safety to stop the aircraft from moving forward unexpectedly in the event of a malfunction.

I would stand in front of the engine facing the prop and yell out, "Switch off, throttle closed." The instructor would repeat my words. We were not ready to start the engine; first it needed to be primed. I had to spin the propeller several times to force fuel into the carburetor and engine fuel lines. To rotate the propeller I would grasp the propeller blade at its trailing edge using the second joints of both hands and smartly snap the prop downward. The prop would rotate on its own through a short arc (not starting) moving to the next position of the engines internal rotation cycle. I had to be aware of my position so that I could move quickly out of the way of the prop in case of malfunction. Three spins should have been adequate for priming.

I'd call out, "Contact, switch on." The instructor would repeat my words. I'd check my footing, grasp the prop and pull down quickly. The engine may start the first time. I had to be prepared to move out quickly. With the engine running, I would stand on the right side of the Cub where the aircraft's door was located in view of the instructor. He would let the engine idle for several minutes to view the gauges. Satisfied, he would motion to me to pull the chocks. I'd pull the cord on the right wheel chock to remove it, and move around the tail of the Cub and repeat the chock removal on the left side. When done, I'd give the instructor a "thumbs up."

The early model Cub had no brakes. It had two main gear wheels and a tail wheel. Airplanes of that configuration were called tail draggers. They needed to be at a good idle speed to start the aircraft rolling, especially if they were on a grass strip. This starting procedure may seem overly complicated, especially when written down. In practice the entire sequence from start to the
70

aircraft getting into the not so wild blue yonder may be ten minutes.

I received no regular pay but was promised free flying lessons. That sounded wonderful. The flight instructors were there to bring in money and fly, fly, fly. Sometimes we would bring them sandwiches and soda while they remained in the airplane and students were shuffled back and forth to the airplane. Late Sunday was the end of the instructors' day, and it was almost sundown. They were tired. Then the manager would ask an instructor, "Can you take the kid up for a lesson?" When I didn't get a lesson, I would go outside the office and cry in frustration.

I finally did get my private pilot's license. I went into the service and that was the end of an era.

# *Hope*

J.C. Strauss

Stella was nervous sitting alone in the booth at Denny's. Since the passing of her husband of thirty-five years, she had gone through several stages of grief. First, the fact that he was gone and not just running down to the store for another six-pack of beer; as much as she disliked his drinking, she now wished that was where he had gone.

Then the anger that he was gone and she was trying to pick up the pieces. Now the final stage, the loneliness of an empty home; the children all married and moved into their own homes and lives. With the passage of time she found ways to cope - learning once more to cook for one; sleeping on the couch so she could try making herself believe that he was sleeping in the bedroom; leaving the TV on all the time so the house did not feel totally empty and quiet.

They had married when she was just eighteen and he was twenty-five. The first few years were rough and the children started arriving much too soon. But they quickly became the joy of their lives. The four boys and two girls made them decide they would move from the small town in Texas to California where the children would have hopes for a better life than they could find in a small town in Texas.

The years went quickly by. He had always planned to see the doctor to check on the small pain in his chest and the shortness of breath when he worked hard. But the pain was always slight and went away quickly.

She often remembered that day as she was sitting at the table drinking coffee while her husband was mowing the backyard. She was watching as he suddenly grabbed at his chest and fell to his knees. The EMT told Stella he was most likely dead by the time he hit the grass.

That was over four years ago. At a friend's encouragement she decided to start dating. Her friend told her she was only fifty-two and looked a few years younger. She had tried several of the on-line dating sites but was always disappointed. The ones that sounded interesting were either overweight or a lot older than their photo.

So here she sat with the red flower in her dark hair and a copy of today's newspaper on the table so Donald would recognize her. She closely watched every man who entered hoping he might be this one and then not that one.

Finally a man entered wearing a gray suit with a red rose on the lapel, a signal to Stella that this was the person she was waiting for. She was relieved and pleased. The photo and description he posted were accurate.

After he had sat down and they had talked for several minutes, she moved her purse from the edge of the table placing it on the bench beside her, a signal to her son who was sitting just a few tables away that she would be okay. But her son remained for the rest of the evening watching as they talked.

They talked for over two hours and agreed to meet at church service Sunday morning and have lunch afterwards. As they left, Donald opened the car door for her and gently held her hand as she sat down behind the steering wheel and said goodnight.

As Stella drove home, she was very pleased with the way the evening had gone and thinking maybe, just maybe there could be hope for the beginning of a new life after all. She just might have the luxury of another loving relationship. Twice in one lifetime? Why not?

# Is That Your Child?

Nancy Graham

Is that your son who can't survive without an
Iphone, tablet, and computer?
Is that your daughter, snuggled in bed, dreaming of
nice clothes, fast food, and summers at the lake?
Most likely, yes.  Not to judge. They belong to you.
Then tell me this
Is that your son, lying crushed by rubble on a
war-torn street in Syria?
Is that your daughter, lying bloody and bruised on a
cot in Calcutta?
Is that your child, sipping dirty water and begging
for food in Bolivia?
Is that your baby, brought dusty and lifeless, to a
Sudan hospital, in the middle of nowhere?
Most likely, not.  Mostly likely, never.

But GOD holds all these children dear,
These children of the earth,
That he values as much as yours.

# A Safe Place to Be

Nancy Graham

Mira lay quietly, feeling the warmth of the summer earth. Pine needles lay under her outstretched fingers. Soft moss touched her bare toes. She was safe for now. She felt a cool breeze. She shivered. The death of the last one frightened her. She closed her eyes seeking peace. Her mind picked up a magic brush full of rainbow colors. She painted a place where there was no death, no fear, and no more broken children.

# *Keep it Real*

Regina Crump

Keep it real, what cha mean?
Keep it natural with my hair
Keep it nappy, curly, gray

Keep it real, what cha mean?
Keep it natural with my skin, no make-up,
no false eyelashes, no lipstick, no color

Keep it real, what cha mean?
Keep it natural with my body, no fake nails,
no push up bras, no slender wear, no high heels

Keep it real, what cha mean?
with my love for others no judgment,
no jealousy, no pretending, no manipulating,
no attitude.

Keep it real about my feelings on poverty
Selfishness, depression, homelessness, loneliness
Keep it real.

When I look in the mirror, I'm cool with what I see.
God is working in me, on me, with me.
What I mean is His Word, His promise
Keeps me real!

# Life's Cruel Jokes

Marge Ramsey

As people age, you expect them to become forgetful about names, where they left their keys, whether or not they took their medicine, etc. But sometimes life has a way of adding insult to injury. Is there even one senior citizen out there who hasn't been tortured by manufacturers? Manufacturers, you say, how so?

When was the last time you struggled to open a tamper-proof package? Just the other day I bought a salad from a fast food restaurant. Anxious to calm the rumbling in my stomach, I pulled on the easy open tab on my salad container. It didn't budge. I'll try my teeth. Nope, that didn't work either. Perhaps I need to risk bodily injury and try prying it open with a knife. After quite a struggle, I broke the seal and was rewarded with a tasty salad. Now I ponder, what is the justification for putting a salad into protective custody?

And it doesn't end there. I buy ink cartridges for my printer that come three to a pack and are sealed with heavy plastic and bullet proof cardboard. I get out the heavy-duty scissors and struggle to cut through the cardboard on the "cut here" line. What did I accomplish? Nothing! Now I can't separate the two layers of cardboard to access the cartridges, which are safely tucked away behind the plastic. I'll get the knife again. Maybe I can use it to pry apart the layers of cardboard. Now I learn the role glue plays in this whole situation. The layers are separated at the point of knife entry, but the glue is holding on for dear life all around the perimeter of the cardboard! Now I am in need of weight lifting classes to build sufficient strength to win the battle over the glue. Again, what is the purpose here?

I don't know the answer to that question, but I do believe that every senior citizen needs a "package entry" kit in addition to a household tool kit. The contents might include, but not be limited to the following:

• Heavy-duty scissors
• Sharp knife
• Band-Aids in case of injury
• Crow bar
• Pliers
• Rubber grippers for stubborn jar lids
• Hair dryer to heat and release glue
• Magnifying glass to read very tiny opening instructions
• Dentist's phone # for appointments to keep teeth healthy & strong
• A list of manufacturers' help line numbers for package entry assistance
• The phone number for a Package Entry Support Group.

Oh wait, I don't think a Support Group exists. But the creation of one is something we might all think about and ban together to make happen. In the meantime, hang in there, senior citizens, you are not alone.


# *Love is Magic*

Pamela Kaiser Lowell

Love is magic
It shines like the sun in a blue sky
Sparkles like the stars on a clear night
Glows like the moon lighting a dark sky
Calms like ripples on a sea
Gives strength and support in difficult times
All is right, peaceful and safe through love

Life is like a song and love is the music
for that song
Listen to the music and always
Keep LOVE in your heart.

# Linda & Margaret

## Linda Moore

I met Margaret in April of 1997, when the Riverside Children's Theater was doing their 40th Anniversary Celebration. Jamil Dada and I were on the Public Relations Board and we decided since the Wizard of Oz was the featured play, we would ask the munchkins to be our guest speakers. I called eight of the remaining munchkins on the telephone. I explained who I was and why I was calling. Meinhardt (the orator) immediately hung up on me. Margaret was the first to agree to come and Jerry Maren was the second. Jerry came by car with his wife Elizabeth (also a midget), since he lived nearby in Los Angeles. Margaret flew in from Phoenix, Arizona because she lived close by in Glendale.

We (my family) met Margaret at Ontario Airport. We were supposed to be there at 3:30 PM, but I was late. The trip started when I rounded up my three children and we all got into our very used white Dodge van and headed off for Ontario. It was a typical Friday afternoon, which meant that there were cars lined up bumper to bumper on the 60 Freeway. I don't know how but I ended up in a field of multi-colored flowers, instead of the

Southwest terminal. I remember getting out of my car and walking down row after row of flowered paths. It seemed like it was taking forever to get where I needed to be. I noticed lots of strawberries and daisies, but no Margaret.

Finally, when it seemed like we had walked a very long time, a little lady appeared. Thank God, she had a sense of humor. Her first words to me were, "You're late. You must be Linda!"

"Yes, I am," I said.

"Well, thank God you showed up. I'm exhausted and was getting kind of scared. You know it's been an hour and a half since I got off the plane. Anyway, let's go. I'm ready!"

So, we get into the family van (all of us). We are just about to take off. I seat belted the boys (Justin aged 5) and Timmy (just turned 7). When, all of a sudden, my car alarm goes off. And is it loud! At this point, I'm very embarrassed and Margaret does not look pleased. I try very hard to make it stop. But I can't seem to do it. Nothing seems to work. It has been at least a half an hour, so I get the Caravan automobile manual out and I do everything it says to do, but that horrible noise continues on and on, nonstop. Margaret is saying, "Let's go, Linda!" But I explain to her that I can't. The car won't move. The car alarm prevents me from driving the vehicle. Until it's turned off, we are stuck in Ontario surrounded by strawberry fields and daisies.

"OK, Linda, I understand.  Can you call your husband?"

"Yes, I can Margaret."

So, I call John who tells me to get out the manual again and "I'll walk you through it.  Now, do exactly what it says."

We do.  But the alarm is still humming loudly and we're not successful at all!  Finally, my son Timmy starts to laugh and all of a sudden there is silence.  The alarm has stopped and there is no sound at all.  Margaret is thrilled.

"Let's go!  I can't wait to get to your house, clean-up, use the john and have a nibble, hee, hee, hee."

We're finally off.  I'm so tired.

"I know you're a nice lady, Linda, but oh I'm beat!"

# Minor Incident
## Edith Nevins

I was sitting in my front yard, trying to find a subject to write about when I noticed a young, African-American lady, parked in her car, on the side street, facing my house.

What would possess Diane Evans to park on an empty side street in suburban, residential Moreno Valley in mid-afternoon, on Monday?

She was sitting alone in the car, a four-door beige car with tinted windows, probably waiting for her boyfriend. This was their secret rendezvous, away from the prying eyes of both family and friends.

She walked over to the passenger side of the car. She appeared to be in her early twenties. In this residential area, there are no commercial stores or other places that could offer assistance for bodily needs. She leaned down against the car and proceeded to pull down her jeans to urinate on the curb.

When she had finished, she pulled her jeans up and looked around to see who was watching, and then walked back to the driver's side of the car and got in.

I became curious, wondering how long she would be parked there. Thirty minutes later, a blue truck pulled up behind her car. The driver, a white, Hispanic male, slammed the truck door, locked it, and walked into the corner house.

Ten minutes later, she drove down the street, made a U-turn, and came back down the same parking spot. She left the driver's seat and walked around to the passenger side of the car and sat down. A young African-American man arrived, sat in the front seat, and drove the car down the street.

The larger significance of this story is that Diane Evans parked on the side street, waiting to meet her boyfriend, who lived down the street. She realized that she could not go into the home of her boyfriend to use the restroom as it might cause an embarrassing situation. She realized that she needed to use the restroom and decided to get out of the car and pee on the curb, looking around to see who was watching. After she was finished, she returned to the driver side of the car, smiling as she sat down.

# *Miracle Worker*

## Mona Lisa Stallworth

"You will feel fulfilled when you do the impossible for someone else."

This was an inscription attached to something; I think it was a tea bag. Somehow what it was attached to does not seem important but the words struck me. They seem to imply that what may be impossible for someone is very possible for another person.

These words caused me to remember a story I was once told. In this story there were a group of hungry people seated around a large pot of delicious looking food and the aroma that was emitted from it made your mouth water.

The people were linked together in such a manner that they were only able to use one hand. Each person was given a spoon in which to scoop up some food from the pot – the problem was the length of the spoon prohibited the person from being able to bring the food-filled spoon to his/her mouth.

Finally after many hours of trying desperately to get the food to their mouths, someone realized that the food-filled spoon could be used to feed the person across from them. Although everyone saw the logic in this and how it could really work, there was much debate about doing it.

Many were concerned whether the one being fed could be trusted. They argued that the one being fed would get their fill and then not feed the feeder. This heated discussion went on for a while before one brave soul spoke up. He said, "I will go first." He was willing to take the risk for he reasoned that not to take the chance would mean they would all surely die of starvation in the midst of this large pot of food. So he began to feed the person across from him.  Then slowly one by one they began to feed each other.  In the end all were fed. See, what appeared to be impossible to do for self was possible to do for another.

I wonder how often are we in a position to do for others what may be impossible for them to do for themselves. I wonder how many times we failed to do the impossible for someone because of fear, self-centeredness, narrow-mindedness, pride, jealousy, stubbornness; I mean you can fill in the blank. We are very good at coming up with reasons and excuses for our lack of action.

Most people believe that only God can do the impossible or perform miracles. I disagree. I believe we can all be miracle workers. To me doing something for someone else that is impossible for them to do is performing a miracle. Miracles do not have to be earth-shattering things. Stopping by a shut-in unexpectedly with a bag of groceries is a miracle to that shut-in. Having the ability as a tutor to get a student to understand a difficult concept is a miracle for that student. Using your gift of encouragement to give hope to someone who is suicidal is performing a miracle.

When you perform these small miracles in someone else's life you will truly feel fulfilled and they are forever grateful that you chose to do the impossible! I would hope that everyone would consider joining me and become a miracle worker in your lifetime.

# My Loud Music
## Ollie Eubany

I live in a three-story apartment building over a mattress store. My street is very quiet and peaceful as well as my one bedroom apartment. I am thirty-three years old and have been living alone for a while now. My former boyfriend left me when he fell in love with another. I find so much comfort in living alone now but it was difficult at first. I am attractive and have gone out again from time to time, but now I enjoy my nights alone. The apartment above me had been vacant for some time. But yesterday it looks like someone has occupied it. I thought that was nice; maybe I can meet a friend.

I peeked through the curtains and saw this man carrying his suitcase up the stairs. He was tall, on the heavy side with hair in dreadlocks. He had an interesting face and I felt we would get to know each other.

When I returned from work that next day he was coming down the stairs. I introduced myself and he said his name was Harvey. I told him if he needed anything he could knock at my door. After two weeks he started playing his Reggae music late at night. It did not bother me at first, but when I met him on the stairs next I asked him to turn his music down a bit since I have to get up early in the morning for work. He did not answer; he just gave me this odd look. That evening after I had eaten and was watching my TV I heard his music. I thought I would overlook it but when I got in bed the music was really loud. I put on my robe and went up, knocked on his door and asked him to turn the music down, please. He slammed the door in my face so I walked downstairs back to my apartment and thought I would call the landlord to complain in the morning. The landlord came around the next day but Harvey must have suspected because he did not play his music until after the landlord left.

This late night loud music continued for weeks and kept waking me up. I was grumpy at work not having a good night sleep. I did not know what to do, since my rent was low and if I moved I would have to pay more than I could afford. I had no witnesses since he played his music only throughout the night. I was at my wits end and every time I opened my door he would open his and call me a bitch and other nasty names.

What I finally did came to me one night when I could not stand anymore. Next morning I did not get up for work, instead I waited till Harvey came down the steps to go out. I hastily ran up to his floor and unscrewed the light bulb in the ceiling knowing that he would not notice since his only focus was on harassing me. He usually came home early so when I heard his footsteps I listened to see if he would replace the light bulb, but he didn't. I waited for some hours. Meantime I pulled out two of my frying pans and a big pot. I greased the bottom of the pots, then, later when he turned up his music I went into the hallway, climbed the steps and put the large pot and the frying pans on each step. I ran back into my apartment, waited a bit, and then dialed his number.

When he answered I told him in a loud voice that the building was on fire. He slammed down the phone and ran down the stairs, but lost his balance when he slipped on my frying pans. He came down on his head and lay unconscious on the bottom landing. I tiptoed around him, retrieved my pots and pans, closed my door and promptly got into bed.

I slept well that night. In fact I did sleep well for some time since there was no more late night music and my jail cell was very quiet.

# My Musical Self
## Cathy Fortin Jenkins

My mother never told me and I wish I didn't know about gravity and what it is doing to my body and soul. For seven decades, gravity has been pushing down on every part of my body. This downward motion is especially evident in my sagging integumentary system or in an everyday word-my skin. I am developing bat wings on my underarms. Camouflage is the answer-no sleeveless blouses for me! No amount of Ponds, Biotherm, or Neutrogena creams can stop the downhill road race on my face. Soon I will have a road map covering my face and neck.

Then there is my musculoskeletal system. It is making strange creaking, cracking, crepitating sounds. Sometimes an unexpected and involuntary groan makes its way from the depths of my being. The invisible xylophonist in my body begins at my knees looking for the correct note up and down my vertebral column.

Then there is the digestive system which also makes all sorts of gurgling, gushing and sometimes embarrassing tooting noises. Different foods affect me in various ways that they never did when I was young and could eat anything.

I suppose that those senior citizens who have

poor hearing are blessed because they can't hear the symphony orchestra of string and tympanum performing in their bodies. I really should not complain, I am fortunate that I still am attuned to the music of my body, still working part time, and can see well with my glasses. I have seen my grandchildren grow into adulthood. I even have two great grandchildren.

Things could be worse. I could be pushing up daisies

# Ode to an Ex-husband

Cathy Fortin-Jenkins

You remind me of a glacier,
a cold and stony block of impenetrable ice.
You made icicles of words
but sometimes,
You uttered things as smooth as
blue velvet.
That's how we stayed hooked.
On top, bright and glistening
a frozen monument to winter
but underneath
grinding, grating, crushing.
pushing and shoving,
leaving wreckage and impressions on the land.
You and your vodka left glacial marks
on our family.
Mighty was our effort to overcome
but we were left with coldness
next to bone.
Your anger was like the iceberg that sank the
Titanic.
We were afloat in the sea,
foundering, grasping for any lifeboat.
Several came along.
You sank.
We survived.

# Old Fashion Recipe for the Soul

Pamela Cockerham

Arise early,
- Heat your oven on your knees. Add 15-30 minutes of prayer.

Gradually turn up the time longer.
- Listen to the Holy Spirit. When your oven has reached a certain temperature; the Holy Spirit will let you know, okay, it's time to come up higher, simmer.
- Add one large cup of peace, unlimited sugar, no calorie kisses.
- Add hugs to family, friends, and love ones.
- Add one large laughter (good medicine)
- At least one phone call per week. Let someone know you thought about them.
- Marinate on the Word, meditate, on the Holy Spirit all day.

Last ingredient
- Season well with Forgiveness, (no worries). You can't have too much seasoning. Forgive all who have hurt or wronged you in any way, past or present, (vengeance does not belong to you). If you can't remember at the time who you left out, rely on the Holy

Spirit. He will bring all things to your mind. Footnote: (Do not allow the devil to dance in your head)
- Use as much forgiveness as necessary to clean out your oven. You will need to continue this in the future.
- Mix all ingredients well.
- Bake with hands raised high and lifted up. Continue all of these steps every day until God calls you home. You're sure to hear, "Well done, my good and faithful servant,

Now you can go and taste, see that the Lord is mmmm good.

Don't forget to share.

This recipe was brought to you by Pamela Cockerham, and inspired by the Holy Spirit.

# *Our Planet*

Phillip Sanchez

In the Life I'm living, I am but on the edge of
history.
Looking at the development of we as
A species.
I'm just not sure if…
We are going to make it
To live on the face of this, our Earth
For as long as we could.
We seem so determined to
Destroy for convenience sake
To destroy for an easier way, or for more.
Beyond all the scriptures of the writings in time
We, we… can't seem to live
In a way that will truly sustain the
Life of this our Planet.

# Overexposure is a Sign of Under Evaluation

Mona Lisa Stallworth

When I was young I thought nothing of showing my body- not outrageously so I just thought that showing some cleavage was no big deal. And of course allowing others to see my backside was just the thing to do. Then I heard a story of a man who without thought showed some visitors all of his treasures, only to have them come back later and rob him.

Now I understood the point of the story but I did not relate it to my dressing. No, it was only when I heard a man say "the world's greatest treasures are covered requiring effort to excavate them!" Then something clicked. He was correct. All of the world's riches-minerals, oil, and precious stones were all buried deep in the earth. They required great effort to excavate them. It hit me; my body is one of my greatest assets yet I had not kept it covered. The exposure of my body set me up to be robbed emotionally, psychologically and physically. Had I valued my body I would have kept it covered and waited for the one willing to put forth the effort to uncover my jewels.

Today I am more modest in my dress. I want that special man to feel like he has discovered a well-hidden treasure. For today I know my true value and I keep my assets covered.

# *The Coming Storm*
Nancy Graham

The rain ping pinging on the window was only interrupted by the banging of a loose shutter. It was the beginning of a severe storm. I heard a familiar meow from outside. Bartholomew wanted in. As I creaked open the old door, he stopped crying and pattered in on soft feet. He was soaked to the bone. I dried the furry cat with his favorite towel and placed him in the armchair. I lit a fire in the old wood stove and the crackle of the burning wood and the purring of Bartholomew distracted me from the coming fury - the tympanic sounds of high winds and torrential rain.

# Point of Light

Pamela Cockerham

I can remember at the age of five, my mom working, my dad lived with us. He played instruments and he was a cook, and a good one, I might add. And there was my Nanny, that's what we called her. She was my grandma; she lived with us until she got her own senior apartment.

I was about thirteen or fourteen. I knew my mom didn't have life skills, but I knew one thing for sure, I was loved. I was not close to my dad as my sister was; he was in the army. There were times I would hear my dad and mom argue, never fight, just argue. I use to close my ears. The sounds made me feel sad inside. When I put my hands over my ears, the sounds would go away. I would pretend to be places where I wasn't - I would travel, or I would visit my best friend Jenell's house, or on the playground where my other friends were. I remember during the week, when my parents would argue, it didn't happen too often, but for me often enough. During the week, it didn't matter because come Sunday morning, Mom would come into our room and wake us up for church.

My mom was my point of light. I had four brothers, and one sister - Starla, Abraham, John, Tomas, and Paul (not their real names.) When it

100

came to me, Mom would wake me, "Sunshine, time to rise and shine." Mom went to church often. Whether she went or not, us kids went. Now my grandma, well, she was in church every Sunday and Sunday nights for BETU. I don't remember what it stood for but I remember looking at the sign on the wall outside of the church. It was wooden and brown, the words carved in white.

My grandma was also my point of light; she taught me that God did love me. I know that my grandma and mom had no example to live by. My mom was an only child. I later learned about a point of light. Days turned into weeks, weeks into months, and one day Mom took us kids aside and talked to us. She said she was filing for divorce; she did not want to stay in the relationship.

My mom and grandma taught me the point of light. They taught me how to treat people, about respect, even when people weren't so nice. There were many people who had a hand in raising me and teaching me the point of light.

My brother was another person who taught me the point of light. He used to build things with his hands and every time he did, he would tell me to come and watch.

He said, "I am helping you for the future. Always pay attention."

So I did. Today he is sixty-one years old and not married, self-taught carpenter. Abraham was my point of light.

I use to volunteer at Riverside Community Regional Medical Center (RCRMC), working the front desk. One day, this man came in.

Someone walked him to the door and said, "Now, this is as far as I am going to take you. Someone will come and help you." As I looked around, everyone walked past him.

Finally I went to him and told him who I was and said, "I will help you. Where would you like to go?" He told me and I took him. He tried to pay me.

"No one would help me, but you did."

"Sir," I said. "This is what I love to do."

Over and over he said, "God bless you. I can't see. I am blind."

I said, "You can't buy care and I care." He was my point of light.

I was blessed with three sons. So caring, so loving, they all look out for me. My youngest, Job, is twenty-six and takes much care of me, calls me every morning and night before bed to make sure I'm okay. One day I had to go to the hospital and a friend called him. He lives in Hollywood. He must have driven to Moreno Valley on two wheels, he got to the hospital so fast. My, my, what a point of light Job is to me!

102

# *Re-entry*

## Mona Lisa Stallworth

Where have the years gone?
It seems like just yesterday, when I was young
and very social.
Where have all the friends gone?
 We used to gather and party until the break of
dawn
What about all the evenings spent laughing,
loving and enjoying each other's company?
Where has it all gone?
Today I look around and it's all new, yet old at
the same time. I look at the same house but it's
not the same.
Though it's full of memories, it still does not feel
the same.
I go to call a friend, but it's not the same
Though we have history together, I cannot seem
to relate.
Where have all the years gone?  Who am I?
When did I cease to be part of my community?
How did it happen?
Little did I know that when I took on my partner
That our world would close in on us.

Slowly over the years we retreated more into
each other.
The family gatherings became fewer
And social gatherings became even more of a
rarity
Now that he's gone what do I do?
How do I re-enter a world I left so long ago?
How do I open up and realize that I have been
given a second chance to explore,
to open up this oyster of a world and pull out my
pearl.
Yes, though I ask where the years have gone
I must realized that I have been blessed to have
Good health to enjoy the days ahead

Though I have asked where are all my friends,
I know those that are gone are in a better place
And I have the good fortune to still be able to
make new friends
Though I have lost my love, I know love is never
really lost.  And the more you love the more it
comes back to you
Though my home is filled with memories of the
past, there is still room to hold new memories
that I still have time to create

My calling old friends are both a source of
comfort and challenge;

Our history gives me a secure place to go and
share yet my long absence has caused a void
My community went on without me.  My
isolation went unnoticed.
Family and friends gathered, laughed and
fellowshipped without me

Thank God for the re-entry points I have been
lead to explore: Yes, all the wonderful
community activities, senior programs,
Volunteering opportunities waiting for me,
clubs and organizations yearning for me to join.
There's karaoke night, turnaround trips and
tourist hot spots bidding for my time.

Then there are always those friends and family
members who are there with their open arms
saying, "Welcome back- we have missed you"
And let's not forget old boyfriends whose flames
have not gone out

# *Reincarnation*
### Rene Walter Madayski

Most major religions promise the souls of their just to dwell after their journey on earth in the nearness of their deity in heaven, paradise, or in Walhalla or the eternal hunting grounds. The religion of the most populous nation on earth, however, teaches the return of all souls into the body of a future being, those of the just into one of a higher social standing, human or animal, and vice versa. Were I to believe in this reincarnation, what new being would I prefer to be, definitely a peregrine falcon. Why, because, along with the Arabian steed and the camel, it is the most venerated and honored animal in the lands of the Fertile Crescent. I would be permitted to die of old age, and not be hunted for my fur like bison, grizzly and seal. I would not be poached for my tusks like walrus, elephant and rhinoceros, not be often mistreated by owners of cats and dogs, supposedly friendly pet owners. Nor would I be shot for meat like antelope and deer, nor bled to death like sheep, goat and other ritually slaughtered animals. On the contrary, I may be adopted by a Bedouin family as their son and honored with all the privileges of a human being. As the only animal in this world I would get a travel passport issued by the State of

106

Dubai, and when traveling from the Emirates, I would have my own seat on the plane next to my Bedouin father who had adopted me as his son, and I would never have to travel in a cage, even as priceless race horses have to do.

I may live from 12-18 years, as a male be worth between $1500-5000, as a female from $5000-18000, and with exceptional hunting qualities up to $80,000. I would be able to fly wherever my interests take me, thus I could soar over areas of present or past historical interests. Not too far from my Emirate homeland I would sail over the Kings Highway where not only caravans traveled, to Aquaba, but also ancient armies marched to their battle destinies, and over Megiddo and Kadesch where Egyptian forces clashed with northern expanding armies on their march south, the Hittites, the Assyrians. My Argus eyes would spot in the mists of the past Narmer unite Egypt, see the step, bent and great pyramids, Abu Simbel, Karnak and Armana being built and the first monotheistic rites being offered, seeing after the ouster of the Semitic Hyksos the foreign settlers being oppressed. The Israelites wandering through Sinai, the Covenant, the settling of Canaan and later the unification of Judea with northern Israel to form a nation under King David to last for 71 years before dividing again under Absalom. However further north I would see the Greek coalition attack Troja which hindered their trade with the Black Sea areas, and much later see Leonidas with his 300 Spartan warriors dying at Thermopylae, but stopping the advance of Achemean Xerxes satrap armies into Greece, and marvel at the eloquent victory of their small fleet at Salamis over the Persian navy. I may also see Alexander the Macedonian, pupil of Aristotle, on his murderous vengeance invasion of the Persian Empire about 700 years later and meeting his arrow on the Indus River, where about 2000 years prior civilizations flourished like Harappa, whose writing today is not yet deciphered. And somewhat later on this approximate route I see ferocious Pashtun tribal warriors battling Maureen Indian armies flooding Afghanistan and in 1834 and 1896 beat British armies trying to add this territory to their Indian empire, as well as routing recently Sowjets and forcing retreat of current invaders and their cohorts. But earlier in Galilee I come across a stonemason, Isa or Joshua, preaching a new order based on faith, whose sayings are later summarized as the Sermon of the Mount. And earlier I see the returning Jews from Babylonian captivity battling with the Samaritans for predominance on Mount Gerizim and lose. I would not miss a new and only truly monotheistic faith being promulgated and sweeping with victorious armies away the older ossified religions of the Greco-Roman world.

108

Sometimes I ascend high into the sky and on the fringes of the continent I observe Neanderthals living out a desolate existence before being wiped out or absorbed by Homo sapiens whose Neolithic hunters finger-painted their horses, bison and mega cats on the cave walls of Lascaux and the Dordogne. And even further north on the shores of the Orkneys I spot Stone Age fishers of Skara Brae, a Neolithic village, older than Stonehenge and the pyramids, throwing their nets.

I may soar high over my beloved fertile crescent lands and spot the tells and jebels not yet excavated, and am cognizant of the new mindset of archeologists not primarily looking for treasure, but for the fabric of ancient cultures and find that despite tremendous differences in material and organizational situations of people then and now all yearned for peace and personal freedom. Personally I would like to expand this to gender equality so sorely missing in the Near East, to equal employment opportunity not based on skin, origin, religious or sexual orientation, freedom of dictatorial regimes or juntas, of no oppression by bolshevism, fascism or exploitation by vulture capitalism, no gas chambers, genocidal carpet or atomic bombing, torture, decade long detention without trial, genital mutilation, forced conversion, LSD experiments on war babies and ethnic cleansing.

Progress is slow now, but the next generation may see more movement in these matters. One must never give up hope. And with this hope in my mind and heart I soar down from above the clouds and land happily on the outstretched arm of my Bedouin falconer father.

P.S. As earthling I stood firmly and inquisitive on all sites mentioned.

As falcon I tried to pierce into the mists of their antiquity.

# September Years

## Anna Christian~

She has reached September years
Watching Time do a number on her.
Sprinkling silver in her dark-brown hair
and dulling the twinkle in her once bright eyes,
hardening the skin on her feet
and brittling her toenails
adding pounds to her already generous frame,
and girth to her spreading hips.
Throwing her into a dark mood filled
with shadows of tombstones and rain.

She has reached September years
Fighting a battle she can't possibly win
Lines drawn all over her face as time advances
sinking a right to her hips, another to her thighs,
and still another to her stomach
Her body rebels but loses
Even gravity pulls her down

~

She has reached September years and
All around her flowers are blooming
Memories parade before her reminding her that once
she was a rose, delicate and desired
Now she is alone and wondering if she'll ever bloom again
But October closes in too quickly.

~

She sinks into October years,
touches the bottom and leaps for air
Her voluptuous birthing body bridging the future

Her smile closeting secret pleasures and understanding
Her face telling her story
rich and empty of regrets
Her arms outstretched, reaching for tomorrow.
With ease she welcomes November and
throws a kiss to December
as September breezes into history!

# Sunrise at Portabello
Al Turnbull

There is something wrong with a lot of people you have to agree. Maybe there is a gene mutation that too many, generally young people have; a defect that makes them think that they are safe from danger and that they can do anything no matter how foolish just to show that they can. Perhaps it's just something that they think no one can do and they can show-off and brag about a stupid accomplishment. They are the persons who think that two minutes on the evening news is worth risking their lives.

Let me tell you what I mean. How often do you see some teenage boys flying through a parking lot on a skateboard or some nut going 80 miles per hour on a motorcycle doing "wheelies"? How about the guy who wanders off a trail in the mountains, without a cell phone, compass, warm clothes or water and it takes 500 searchers a week to locate him? Some people are dumb! Think about the young couple in a rowboat hoping to sail from San Francisco to Samoa?

Old people are not exempt from foolishness, not many of them, because most chance takers are dead or maimed before achieving any elder status. An example is the old woman who every year or so attempts to swim from Cuba to Florida. She gets her brief notoriety along with cramps, hypothermia, and jellyfish stings.

Now I hate to admit it but I have to say that members of my family, not really my family exactly, rather, my in-laws; My wife, her parents and her mother's parents, all participate in a behavior that, sooner or later, I am positive, is going to kill all of them along with innocent people who accept a dinner invitation to their house.

I was nervous of course, when Jodie and I had just started dating and she asked me to meet her parents and have dinner with them. Nervous sure, but if I had only known, I would truly have run for my life. My association with her would have been terminated and my future children would have a sane mother different from the one who comes from a home where everyone might be exterminated at any meal they eat.

Innocent as I was, but cautious, as I had always been since infancy, I went over to her home where I met her family. Ingratiating people they are indeed, just the outstanding sort of souls that

114

detective fiction writers portray as the actual culprits in their novels, the ones you would never suspect. Yes, my wife's family are "salt of the earth," wonderful neighbors (as long as they don't drop a casserole off sometime), calm, polite, likeable, taxpayers, careful drivers—the very ones you would least identify as potential killers.

My wife is aware now, of course, of my apprehension, and she promises that she will never endanger the children or me; and I truly believed that, except what if! What if she becomes careless, disregards my fear, what if she reverts to the cooking instilled in her by her mother and her grandmother? Just between you and me, there have been times when I have abdominal pains, sometimes a little lightheadedness, or nausea, after she has served spaghetti for dinner. Might she have met someone else and wants me gone? Has she taken out a life insurance policy on me? It is an awful thing to live in fear of your wife. The sweet woman, you love so deeply, who cares for you so devotedly, and who is the mother of your adorable children.

My dread heightened about a year ago when her grandfather died. True, he was pretty old and not in the best of health, but his passing was a shock, especially to me. The death certificate lists liver and kidney failure as the cause of his passing. I suggested an autopsy but the family demurred. He was cremated so no evidence remains of anything in his system that might have exacerbated his organ failures.

No, I don't truly believe that my wife or her parents kill people intentionally. I have to think that for there is no reason for me to think otherwise; but, and here is where I am most afraid—what if they do so unintentionally?

April and early May, the rainy months here, are the times that I worry constantly, because factors that heighten the danger then are present. What do those good citizens do then? I'll explain: They own some land, not much, outside the city—it used to be an orchard, but many of the trees have died and were cut down, with decaying stumps left.

What grows on that rotting wood? Well, of course ants and termites, and beetles abound there, but what else? Yes, fungi, wild mushrooms, all sorts of puffballs, toadstools, buttons, shitake, envoi, portabella.

My wife and her parents carry a picture book that points clearly (to an expert) what must be avoided, but her people have been harvesting mushrooms for years so they know, at least, they will bet their lives and those of anyone who comes to eat with them that they know what is safe.

Now I'm certain that they did not intend to murder Grandpa. Perhaps he did have failing organs, or maybe a small bit of mirasmius oreades was too much for the sick old fellow, but was tolerated by the rest of them. I never eat very much when we go to dinner at my wife's parent's place and I have to say when I wake up the next morning after eating there it is that IT IS GOOD TO BE ALIVE.

# The Burning of an African City

Ollie Eubany

Bombs are exploding everywhere
Even as I sleep
Rockets bursting in air
My senses scatter
Even as I sleep
People running to escape ensuing fires
Fires leaping to ensnare escaping people
The agony of screaming children
Even as my own awake terrified
The screaming children
Conflagration, explosions and shrapnel
The dead and dying.
Suddenly galvanized, I race to cram
belongings into waiting vehicles
Child on my knee
Another crouching on the floor.
Ahead hundreds, perhaps thousands of vehicles
cover
Existing roads, walkways, pathway to Heaven.
There is no escape
We will surrender or burn with the city.

118

# The Canine Keepers' Pledge

Marcia Hill, CMG

"I COMMIT MYSELF TO THE TASK OF BEING A GREAT DOG OWNER. I WILL DEDICATE MY TIME, EFFORT, LOVE, AND FINANCES SEEING TO MY ANIMAL'S NEEDS. I WILL PURSUE KNOWLEDGE, BECOMING WELL INFORMED, EXERT DILIGENCE GETTING NECESSARY TRAINING, PROVIDING A SAFE ENVIRONMENT INCLUDING HOUSING, PROPER NUTRITION, AND REGULAR GROOMING PROCEDURES FOR ITS HEALTH AND COMFORT"

*Written with the hope that dog owners, or potential dog owners, will read the Canine Keepers' Pledge.*

The age of the dog, whether purchased, adopted, rescued or received as a gift is not of much importance. For the best results follow the pledge, and pour on the love. Bonding and developing mutual respect between you and your canine friend will be very rewarding for years to come.

First, reading about purebred dogs can be not only informative, but also great fun! There are so many different breeds, and examining their history of origin and their intended uses can be quite enlightening. Actually, you might become addicted to the pursuit! The American Kennel Club publication, first a book, now is on the World Wide Web for all to see. You will find ancient drawings, histories, pictures, explanations of anatomy, and terminology that will have you taking a longer look at your canine companions than ever before.

The table of contents will certainly guide you through the Groups, which there are seven, and all of the breeds of dogs listed in each one. For example, Working dogs work, hounds usually hunt and track, Toys range from tiny to smaller breeds. Do you get the idea? The terminology and glossary sections describe and name unique things like ear shape, size and carriage, eyes, tails, and head type is a huge area to investigate. If you are thinking, why? Try figuring out your wonderful mixed or designer breed companion without some form of canine roadmap. Some answers to your questions pertaining to appearance, colors and markings, traits and temperament, even how a dog might jump or walk, will be obvious from the variety in its gene pool. Imagine that!

Your Pledge addresses a commitment to keep your furry friend well groomed, which is vitally important. No matter what the breed, they all have some form of hair or coat on their bodies. There are a few exceptions, the hairless varieties, such as the Chinese Crested, the Xoloitzcuintli, better known as the Mexican Hairless. Still, their skin needs attention. The beauty of the hairless dogs is no brushing needed! Human tendencies seem to desire something to stroke that is warm, cuddly, and fuzzy. Remember, that all of the different types of coat do shed for various reasons. It could be seasonal, natural to the breed, poor diet, and chronic disease of the body, skin or parasite infestation. These are the things to be aware of and take some form of action to correct.

Whether you've just gotten a young puppy or adopted a grown dog, coat care is constant just like your head of hair. Understanding this prior to your selection of a pet, or just keeping up with the one you have, should be thought out carefully. If the pet has a relatively short coat, you might consider doing the coat maintenance yourself. Have fun!

If your choice is covered from head to toe with some form of hair, wiry, wooly, bushy, or silky, you will need some knowledge, skills, proper equipment, and a lot of patience. Do not wait very long, because there will be trouble with which to deal with. Read up on simple routine instructions on the general care of your animal's coat, or you and the pet need introduction to a Certified groomer.

Get references from neighbors and friends that are happy with their pet services. This is your friend and the care you seek not controlled by distance or price. If you fail your duties, it can get expensive to have someone else correct the coat problems.

As is often stated, "A word to the wise is sufficient."

# *In the Deep Forest of my Childhood*

Nancy Graham

In the deep forest of my childhood, down where the sun barely peeks through the trees, and where the smell of rotting leaves permeates the air and the birds rarely chirp, I stand.

Down where the moisture is deep into the soil and decaying little animals cling to forgotten leaves, I walk slowly, holding my cane. I try to avoid fallen branches and sharp rocks that can pierce my shoes.

I finally see the clearing nestled inside heavy bush. There is a tree, I remember, with my initials and those of my brother. We often hid here from our drunken father.

Many tears were spilled upon this sodden ground. Many hours waiting in fear, my brother and I. I see a rusty pocketknife that belonged to my brother still stuck in the tree. I leave it.

I don't stay. I leave these memories behind, walk up the rise and feel the warmth of the afternoon sun.

# The Closet

### Anne Hendricks-Jones

She knew he wasn't home. She had only intended to walk pass his brownstone on East 87$^{th}$ Street as she'd done every day for two weeks. This time, however, she just had to see what the old apartment looked like. Had he made any changes or were things still the same? Had he gotten rid of the gifts she'd given him, the Ming vase and signed baseball, or were they still in their designated places? She had waited two hours in a line to get A-Rod to sign that baseball and he had admired the vase, on one of their many walks up 5$^{th}$ avenue. She just had to know the answers, so she took out the key on its soft rabbit foot key ring he had given her. She always loved to caress its gentle softness. She should have returned it but couldn't bear to part with it and he didn't ask for it, so she didn't. The key slid easily into the well-oiled lock.

She walked into the foyer and embraced the welcoming smells of well-polished wood and masculine cologne. He was everywhere. The banister on the stairs leading up to the second floor and the molding around all the doorways of all the rooms, as well as the wall paneling in the library were all this deep, dark, masculine brown.

Everything was meant to appeal to masculine sensibilities. The furniture was heavy, strong, and over-stuffed, the way he liked it. The library held wall after wall of shelves of his favorite books and in the center of it was a massive pool table with balls in the triangular rack, ready for play. She noted his huge arm chair in its normal place and with a quick intake of breath saw the smaller arm chair that she had begged him to buy for her, still there as well. But, someone else's tennis shoes were under it now. She backed out of the library as if she had walked in on a conversation she was not meant to hear.

Quickly, she mounted the richly carpeted stairs. She would just take a quick peek in the master bedroom to see if the vase and signed baseball were still there and then she would go. She reasoned that it meant he still had feelings for her. She walked into the bedroom and immediately caught whiffs of his favorite cologne, Old Spice. It wrenched her heart, she missed him so. It almost made her forget why she was there, so steadying herself, she moved to the other side of the bed and saw them, both the Ming vase and the signed baseball. She had just reached out to caress the vase's beautiful, blue, raised and etched surface when she heard the front door open below, and a multitude of steps clump up the stairs. Panicked and without thinking, she looked for a place to hide and noticed the walk-in closet. Hurriedly, she let herself in, moved the dirty clothes hamper, and hunkered down behind it, hoping he wouldn't notice, were he to enter.

The footsteps seemed to stop at the bedroom door giving her hope that they wouldn't come in but it was not to be. She discerned the sounds of heavy kissing, the noises of enjoyment, and her hopes were dashed. The bedroom door opened and the sounds of laughter and of un-zippering of clothing sent her even deeper into dismay. Then, the bed creaked loudly and more noises of enjoyment and rhythmic activity emanated from that direction and she knew she was going to be in the closet for the long haul. Oh such screaming and yelling, and "Yes! Yes!!" and "Touch me there!" and "Oh my God!" and "You're the BEST!" and "No one's ever done it like YOU!"

It all began to make her angry as she sat scrunched among the odors of dirty clothing, Old Spice, mothballs, and shoe leather and the hot tears of disgust and embarrassment flowed incessantly. "He never said any of those things when WE made love." Finally, after what seemed like hours, the house was silent again and she crept out stiffly from behind the basket and listened. The soft snores of satiety wafted back. She quietly opened the closet door, glancing at the two protagonists, deeply asleep in their nakedness and sprawled across the bed. Grabbing the Ming vase and signed baseball, she quietly and slowly went out of the room and down the stairs. Noiselessly, the front door opened and she was out in the street again, free at last from her obsession. She gave the ball to a passing teenager, who could not believe his good fortune. She let the vase drop to the concrete sidewalk, where it crashed into a thousand pieces. She, however, was whole, again.

# The Home Alarm

Anne Hendricks-Jones

In the mid-eighties, some years after we bought our house, there were many stories in the newspapers and on TV about home invasions. The ones that made it on the six o'clock news were brutal. Everyday, it seemed that a house with people still in it was being broken into, the people brutalized and often killed, and their belongings taken, in broad daylight, in some cases. If you weren't careful, you would end up believing that it happened more frequently than it really was. TV will do that, and so the more I heard of these incidents, the more frightened I became. I took as many precautions as I could, putting locks on all the windows and doors, purchasing a security door for the front, doing security checks before we left the house, leaving a light on in the house, and installing halogen lights on the back and front porches, and so on, but to no avail. I still lay in bed at night, wide awake, listening at all the night sounds, the creaking of the house, the dripping water faucet, the hiss of the toilet. Any sound put me on edge as I waited for someone to break in through our back door or for the Night Stalker to come through the bedroom window. I even had a knife on my bed stand, next to the alarm clock. A gun was out of the question. Statistically, more people were killed with their own guns than in any other situation so I wasn't going to contribute to my own demise.

One particularly stressful evening of watching yet another report of a home invasion, I went to bed and commenced my now very distressful ritual of listening to the various night sounds and imagining what could happen. The thoughts would not stop and I started trembling and went into a cold sweat. I was so miserable and I didn't know what to do, just lying there, when all of a sudden, a song filled my head.

Que sera, sera

Whatever will be, will be

The future's not ours to see

Que sera, sera
What will be, will be[1]

As sung by Doris Day, this song enveloped me, relaxing me, making me forget my anxieties until I finally went to sleep. And boy! It was the best sleep I had had in many months. I woke up refreshed and never again worried about a break-in. That doesn't mean I didn't continue security checks and doing everything possible to thwart a robbery but whenever I felt myself getting anxious, I just remembered "Que Sera, Sera" and could then move on. Now tell me, how could this NOT have been the work of a guardian angel? I hadn't thought of Doris Day in many, many years, back in high school times, when TVs were still black and white. And then, on top of that, out of the blue, my husband purchased a home alarm system. My husband doesn't do spontaneity or on a whim and he had poo-poo'd me when I told him of my concerns. This had to be the work of an external force. Thank you Doris Day and my guardian angel!

[1] Ray Evans and Jay Livingston, composers, 1956

# The Old Man

J.C. Strauss

The young boys laughed at the old man who seldom shaved or had clean clothes to wear. He was often seen around town as he slowly shuffled from Dumpster to Dumpster looking for items that could be sold to pay for his daily meal. Sometimes he would be seen sitting on bus stop benches and the people would shake their heads and rush quickly by as he talked to friends they could not see. They laughed loudly when he would jump or dive to the ground at the sound of an engine backfire or a firecracker sound that was thrown by unsympathetic children and grown men.

Every morning, soon after the little old diner opened located not far from his one room shack in the poorest part of town, he would arrive for his daily breakfast.

For many years he was seen by those who said he was crazy and hurried past. Those that took the time to stop and ask if they could help him in any way, he would always reply, "Thank you. The Lord takes care of me."

Then one cold winter's day he was missing from the little diner and after a few days the owner of the diner and a policeman arrived at the unlocked door of the old rundown shack. When they entered they found him lying on his little cot with a look of peace on his lifeless old wrinkled face.

While removing his meager possessions, they found, lying face down in a drawer, a Navy Cross Medal with a "V" for valor and a copy of the citation letter stating that in 1942 he had been a member of the U.S. Marine Corps forces in the Philippines. After the surrender of the American forces on Corregidor and during the Bataan death march, he managed to escape captivity and for the next four years fought the Japanese in the jungles of the Philippines.

When they went to bury him next to his mother and father who had passed prior to 1945, they found a hero's marker that stated to their surprise that he had not survived the Bataan death march of 1942.

# The Park Bench

Anne Hendricks-Jones

He had just had the most ferocious argument with his wife that he could possibly remember. He had to leave the house or scream, so he went for a walk to cool off, calm down, and reflect upon his next steps. His left arm started to ache, and rubbing it, he arrived at a bench in the park down the block, and sank down upon it. The pain in his arm began to pound, and on top of that, so did his head, but he hardly noticed. He felt so bad that he had yelled at the love of his life. Such a silly, silly argument: whether or not to purchase a new bed. He thought that the one they had was just fine, but his wife wanted a new one. She said the old one hurt her back. So why not just give in and allow her to purchase it? Because, he had given in so much these past few years: the new car for their live-in daughter, financing yet another business for their ne'er do well son, private boarding school for the twins, and the loss of several important clients to a younger employee, at work. There wasn't much money left for a decent retirement and he was the only one bringing it in. The high-pressured selling of commodities was the pits. He really should quit and find something easier to do. The stress was

133

driving him to drink. Why, why, why didn't he insist that his wife get a job and take some of the pressure off?

He was so deep in thought that he didn't notice the strange woman standing in front of him.

"How y'all doin'?" she said to him.

She was a youngish-looking Black woman. Pretty, he thought, but dressed kind of non-committal, neither sexy nor poorly. He was doing just fine but he wasn't going to tell her that. He looked back down at his lap, hoping she was talking to someone else or, would go away and leave him to his thoughts.

"How y'all doin'?" she said again, this time a tad more loudly.

'Good Lord,' he thought. 'Is she going to rob me?'

Then he remembered he'd left the house without his wallet so with that relieving thought, he looked up at her, then around the area, left, right, and back, to see if maybe she was talking to someone else. There was no one else, of course, but when he looked back at her, she wasn't there. Instead, she was sitting right next to him.

"That's better!" she said and breathed a sigh of relief. "These shoes are fabulous but they are killing my feet!"

Looking down, he saw she had on the most unorthodox and fantastical golden, glittery, almost shimmering high heel pumps. At first he thought he saw little wings flapping from the heels, but when he blinked and shook his head, his painful head, and looked again, they were gone. Now he knew the stress was getting to him. His focus returned to her face.

She was looking at him, also, and replied, "Yeah, I know. They don't actually go with my outfit. But what are you gonna do?" as she shrugged. Then she asked once more, gently, "How y'all doin'?"

"I'm so tired" he replied. "My arm hurts like hell and it has been a really nerve-wracking day. How was your day?" he asked, more out of rote than genuine interest.

"So kind of you to ask," she said, not seeming to notice. "As soon as I give my aching feet a rest, I have one last job to do, and then I'll be done."

She was so easy to talk to and before he knew it, he was confessing his boorish behavior and pigheaded ideas. He even talked of his sister, his beautiful Emily, whom he had loved but lost to

135

cancer. She too, had a penchant for outlandish and uncomfortable shoes. She would have adored the ones this lady had on. He couldn't believe how they shimmered. As they chatted and the minutes passed, he began to notice that the woman herself began to shimmer, brighter and brighter, and even began to look very, very familiar.

"Emily! Is that you?" he questioned with a sharp intake of air as he stood up, in disbelief. "But I thought you were…!" and then it dawned on him. The painful arm and pounding head, although no longer noticeable, were signs of stroke. He was dead and his beloved Emily had come to take him home. Surprisingly, he felt no regrets, only joy and happiness at one journey's end and another beginning. He turned towards the bench. There, his mortal self remained, head bowed and lifeless. He turned towards Emily. She was standing, now, with her hand stretched out towards him, beckoning him. He hurried to take it and together as the shimmering engulfed them both, they walked towards the glorious light

# The Value of Work at an Early Age
Stan Corella

At age 13 I was in the 8th grade and getting ready to transition into a new private school. My parents struggled to make ends meet and they had a lot on their plate. I realized that if I was to continue private school I would need to help out my family. I became somewhat of a hustler.

I learned how to earn a dollar and do whatever I needed to do in order to learn about saving a dollar. I became close to merchants, sales persons, retail clerks as well as local delivery persons within our community. I would help clean, sweep, bake bread and secure delivery items that were being delivered. It was a unique time of my life and I met some very special people. I guess you can say that it was the beginning of what was to come in my future.

As time went on, I became a young man with actually no real plan in life. I was always willing to take a chance in whatever job I could get. Of course, I was never broke; I bought what I needed and helped my family, as did my older brothers, to make ends meet. My parents worked yet really never made high income. I learned that opportunity is there for the taking, learning is there for the asking and consistency develops into rewards with dedicated planning. I realized that action with ethics and helping others opens opportunities to no end.

# Traveling to West Africa by Ship

Ollie Eubany

I had booked passage on the Oti River, a cargo ship of the Black Star Shipping Line of Ghana, West Africa. I was booked to sail from New Jersey pier on February 1971, bound for Nigeria. The Civil War in Nigeria had been over for a year and my 5 years old daughter Laura, and I were returning to Nigeria. I had been in New York for over a year and had been working as a secretary at NBC TV in Rockefeller Center. I had been living with my older brother and his wife in Queens, New York and now he was driving us to the pier in New Jersey where the ship was docked. When we arrived we were told the ship would be in port for another three days. I had sent ahead five steamer trunks to the ship earlier that week and they were already on board so I told my brother that I would stay on board.

We were shown to my cabin by the purser and I noted that most of the crew were Ghanaian. The next morning, at breakfast I met the other passengers, one was a Ghanaian, Tony who had just graduated from college and was returning to Ghana. He said he had been in the US for four years and was returning with his new car, which was in the ship's hold. The other passenger was a Nigerian woman, Irma, who was married to a diplomat at the consulate in New York City. She was with her two sons, one the age of my daughter, and the other two years younger.

To my surprise I was woken up that morning to the motion of the ship; we were on our way, and I was so glad I did not go back to New York yesterday. All that day and the evening the ship was going through a storm. That next morning Tony, my daughter and I were at the breakfast table but Irma and her boys were too sick to leave their cabin. Before I could get up from the table the boat started rolling heavily. My daughter said she wanted to throw up so we rushed downstairs to our cabin. On the way I met the purser and he said we were heading for Canada and the weather was pretty bad since we were going through a storm.

"Canada!" I shouted. "I thought we were going to West Africa!" He said this was a cargo ship and it can make stops on the way at any time wherever there was cargo.

As soon as we got in the cabin my daughter started throwing up her breakfast, and then I started to get sick to my stomach and my head was bursting. I could not help my daughter so I rang the bell for the steward and when he came I said, "Tell the purser I want to fly to West Africa. Get me off

140

this ship!"

The steward said we would reach Halifax, Canada tomorrow morning, and then he gave us tablets to take. We both slept till the next morning and when I woke we were docked in Halifax and we felt better. Everyone was at the table in the dining room and Irma said we could get a taxi to the mall to shop after we had eaten. We got off the ship and hailed a taxi. The taxi driver enthused over the new Canadian Prime Minister Trujillo and his wife the whole time he was driving us to the mall.

That afternoon when we sailed the waters were very calm and we were not sick again. Irma and I spent our days eating and sleeping and staring at the ocean while the children ran around the deck. We reached Monrovia, Liberia and with Irma's influence we were able to get a car and driver from the Nigerian embassy to drive us around the town. We stopped at one shop owned by a Lebanese to have ice cream. I noted that the currency they used was old worn American dollars. Next port of call was Free Town, Sierra Leone and again we had a car and driver and toured that city. Then we went to see the famous Fordham Bay College, which was the first university in West Africa.

I was looking forward to touring Ivory Coast, which was the next port of call, but was told next morning that the crew had unloaded their cargo all night and we were now on our way to Senegal.

When we reached Dakar, capital of Senegal, we again had a car from the Nigerian Embassy and toured the town and the market place. I noted the very tall slim and very black Senegalese men, very regal and the women in colorful and beautiful Bubbas with matching head ties, some carrying babies on their backs.

Next morning we were in Accra, Ghana. Everything came to a complete halt on board as most of the crew were home. Many of them left the ship. Then as we were going to the dining room I saw this long line of men in front of the cabin four doors from mine. The door of the cabin opened and a man walked out and I saw this large women lying on the bed. The next man went in and closed the door. I wondered if the captain knew he had a bordello on board. Later at the dining table the women sat across from me, so I guess everyone knew what was going on.

After one week I asked the purser when was the ship leaving port. He said he did not know since most of the crew had gone to their homes but he promised to find us another ship that would go to Lagos, Nigeria. Finally they booked me on another ship, the Birim River, Black Star Line and I watched as they removed my five steamer trunks from the hold, but later that day they brought them all back with no explanation. We were now in Ghana for two weeks when it was confirmed we

142

would in fact board the Birim River that day bound for Lagos. I then watched them take my trunks to the other ship and we boarded. My daughter and I were given two adjourning staterooms. The ship then left port but pulled into another city in Ghana and lots of people boarded the top deck of the ship. They were refugees leaving Ghana because of severe hardship in their country and were going to Lagos. Now we could not walk around the deck since there were so many people and small children everywhere along with their loads and foodstuff.

We finally arrived in Lagos, Nigeria a few days later. We had been sailing for thirty-five days.

# *What About That?*

## Marcia Hill

Non-fat, low fat, whole fat printed on the bottle of milk.
So what about that?
Everything luscious, creamy and rich,
Not to consume according to the pitch,
Dieticians say take your vitamins A, D, E, K, need
forbidden fat help do that,
Solid or liquid we just want to mix it,
Tasty flavors atop, under, or blended through to fix it
For me and you,
Roasting, baking, frying too makes it tastier, it's true,
It can't be denied all of the sources, cream, butter, lard,
olives, grapes, nuts, and
some flowers,
Give the recipe more delicious power,
Paint the flapjacks, fry the chops, drizzle the salads, lighten
the coffee,
They all add a lot,
M. D.'s agree, "No eat the fat" to save your heart,
Scientist confirm your brain needs fat,
Now what about that?
One hundred calories contained in a spoon,
From what is said will one day send you to the moon,
To live with good eats that can't be beat,
Indulged with care and keep moving on your feet!
Now what about that?

# What Do You Like About Growing Older?
## Marcia Hill

This is a great question and my first inclination was to make a statement that goes like this, "that I do not have to start the learning process of the experiences of living my life." In other words I've already been there and done that. What a relief! The future is always uncertain, but the roads already traveled make for a smoother ride.

Childhood was not a picnic, marriage ended up rather disastrously, motherhood was a learn-by-the -hour sometimes exhausting challenge, divorce was like a horror movie, keeping financial stability was a roller coaster ride and maintaining my sanity through it all gave me gray hair!

If you are feeling sorry for me about now and thinking oh this poor woman, what happened in her life that makes her memories so bleak? Now that I am old enough to have heard other peoples stories, I realize that a whole bunch of people have gone through the same scenario, not just me. Looking at it a little further, some didn't do as well as I did. Some kids were foundlings, some women never had neither the bliss or disappointment of marriage, there are lots of childless marriages and many

145

couples have not been blessed with normal healthy children. I thought about some of the movies I've seen some marriages end up with murder. Those born with silver spoons in their mouths often times lose them and many individuals end up either in a mental institution or prison.

Now look at me, having come close to all of the above and not wanting to look back at those times except to type a few simple words in a writing class, I am elated about my current existence. All of those roads well traveled through thick and thin have made me a winner and survivor, rather a champion of the life experience. I go to bed with a thank you prayer and awake with another one. I have the time to observe those coming along that same old road of life and if they were willing to listen, I might be able to get them past some of the thicket. It is always easy to except the bliss but we all need a little help with the difficult times that challenge us, especially in our youth.

Maybe the grand plan is for each generation to have no map for life and their individual pursuits always seem unique only to themselves. My love affairs were so different that I needed to write about them.

After listening to Dr. Laura and watching daytime shows on TV like Jenny Jones, Montel, Jerry Springer, and Oprah, my experiences that troubled me seem trite.

The older that I get the sillier all of the nonsense seems. There is so much more to appreciate than the competitive accomplishments of a bigger, better wedding than your best friends, or a good looking stud for a husband, the karat count on an engagement ring and where you spent your honeymoon. The real prize comes when you celebrate your twenty-fifth or fiftieth wedding anniversary. The test of time through life and its vast amount of scenes played by the many actors are the best stories. There is no loneliness for me in the pursuit of life and I have learned to profit from not only my mistakes but others' pitfalls as well.

In my late seventies now, watching my children manipulating the paths of their lives, guess what ... history is repeating itself again. I don't suffer from too many aches and pains for I have not abused my body totally and have always given it good fuel. My kids seem to be falling apart a little earlier than I did; their lives all stressed out with today's fast pace and keeping up with the Jones's. I often times think that they are growing older faster than I am, aches, pains, gray hair, glasses, high blood pressure and all. They come to me for advice and I offer my wisdom that has been accumulated from the past. They listen and give warm hugs and kisses, but how much of it they really use is the big question. In time their children will do the same thing. Maybe I'll be around to witness some of that as I rock in my chair and drift off into dreamland now and then. Some one of them will plant a tender kiss on my nodding forehead awakening me momentarily and I'll just chuckle softly and smile, delighted to have grown much older, happy to be alive and content in my soul.

# When A Son Mentions His Father

Regina Crump

You might hear it when he's little and he'll ask, "Where is my dad?" You might hear him say as a boy, "I'm going to be like my dad." As a young man, you might hear him ask, "Mom, don't talk bad about my dad anymore."

When your son has no connection, makes no connection with his father, you might hear him say, "I will never be the man my father was to me with my child."

There is a sigh of relief that as a mother, you have set a good example as a loving parent, but when your son mentions his father, you hope with all your heart that because there is absence, that you've shown love never dies.

# Will You Choose Heaven or Hell?

Patsy Seo

We are faced in our lifetime with immense progress. We have opportunities for Heaven on Earth or total annihilation. Let us make the right choices.

My bird bit me on Monday, 4-14-2014. He is nearly 50 years old. I read that Amazon parrots tend to become aggressive when they mature and that is the reason that many bird trainers refuse to breed their birds.

I know that he bit me because he was not getting what he wanted any other way. I had gone out to breakfast with Charles and bought a taco salad with shredded beef. I often have steak for breakfast, just me, the bird, and Evelyn's two dogs. I took his food dish out of his cage and sat it by my plate and was going to give him some of my shredded beef. The parrot was watching me do this. I suddenly saw and remembered the big scoop of guacamole that was mixed in with the shredded beef. I also remembered that avocado is poisonous to birds so I just returned the food dish to the bird's cage. When I grabbed his cage to move it back to the corner, he displayed. Displaying is a sign of emotion. I know he loves me and has displayed for me many times before. Immediately, while still displaying he grabbed hold of my finger hard. I call this biting. He caused a good bit of blood and pain.

There is a continuum between love and hate. As I think of the mating of tigers and the aggression of my bird, I think there may be a continuum between how they are expressed as wedded bliss or violent rape. God gave us free choice. To leave the responsibility of children under seven to make the right choice is a form of child abuse. They must first be taught to choose correctly. This certainly applies to the expression of emotions.

As people mature they normally learn to express and fulfill their emotions in a civilized manner. Some animals such as the German shepherd may become more mature in this respect than most people. We say the dog is domesticated. We say that some animals such as the Hyena and my bird are not.

Personally, I would say that serial killers are not. They lack empathy or spiritual growth, even though they can behave properly following all the nuances of politically acceptable speech and behavior. Other people show empathy and sensitive emotional behavior but fall short when it comes to "politically acceptable speech and behavior."

The Dingo and Pit Bull have returned from

domesticated to basic savage kill or be killed behavior.

We ask soldiers to return temporally and switch back when the need has passed. This is only possible theoretically. In my opinion it causes PTSD post-traumatic stress disorder. In my opinion one does not mature spiritually overnight any more than one matures physically overnight.

I think the big solution to most of the serious predicaments of our time is a change of focus. Look at it this way. Our current focus is the "Bottom Line" which is just money. A few people focus on the pursuit of happiness, which is just the body and life itself. Only a few rare individuals are listening for God's rule on Earth as He does in Heaven, which is necessary for the spiritual growth and even survival. Isn't it obvious that Post Traumatic Stress Disorder is caused by the conflict between the spirit and military programmed behavior of its victim?

# *Your Words Betray You*

## Patsy Seo

We are faced in our lifetime with immense progress. We have opportunities for Heaven on Earth or total annihilation. Let us make the right choices. How about communication? When and what is enough? I have made some bad choices. I have survived and done as well as I have because my parents made my home a miniature Camelot. I had all the advantages they could give me. My discipline was always firm but fair. I attended school, church and college with their support. We never missed Church. My mother was the Sunday school superintendent. My mother was always in the home. She did not work. I can still feel her watching out the kitchen window as I walked to high school. The town had an excellent gossip network and nothing got pass my mother.

Few of today's young people have those advantages. The computer has promised more communication. Meaningful communication is not always the result. Some people hug their laptops. PC's can be very helpful and good intellectual company, but can they replace a mother's warm protective arms?

I love music. Music alone is meaningful

communication. I can feel it lift my soul as it speaks the things of Spirit that can never be communicated with just words.

You only heard noise? You'd rather listen at a busy intersection to the sound of traffic? The motorcycle screaming as it stops and the policeman blowing his whistle as emergency vehicles race by?

I was lucky to be brought up in a Camelot of my parent's making. She did not give a day or time and nothing about what should or would occur. Is it more important to have an open truthful exchange of ideas or be "Political Correct?"

I was brought up in "Brief and to the Point" as the way. My first encounter with "The polite Form" was when we lived in Germany. The salesmen there did not stop by and leave a flyer. The application for a telephone in Germany was at least ten pages long. I sat translating for a couple that wanted to adopt a baby in Germany for more than an hour. The woman interviewing the couple talked for hours and managed to ask no pertinent questions and relay very little information. She said they would be visited later by a social worker to make sure the child was in a good home. The people I consider family and friends let me talk all day, sometimes.

Those are good days. Time wasters and a big luxury, but good.

The Politically Correct world we live in today is

154

poverty stricken by comparison. How many people have been caught by the media bending the truth to manipulate others into doing what they want? The media claims free speech and uses it to criticize. Always negative things are reported. Rodman did a wonderful thing to make friends with North Korea's President. He had to retreat to alcohol rehab to get away from the press's crucifixion. Smart guy. They even chased him down there. Fortunately the place was pretty secure, so their harassment was limited by the rehab staff. Every little slip up of good and useful men is reported and blown out of proportion while the news we need never makes it to the surface.

I like the "Fiddler on the roof" especially the song "If I were a wealthy man." He would biddy biddy boop all day long if he were a wealthy man. Yes, I am a wealthy man. I am enjoying it.

I learned a lot from the "gossip" of my mother with her friends. She had to hide her pants in the smokehouse after her first menstrual cycle. She was careful to tell me everything she knew about sex. My girls could probably have explained the facts of life to her before they went to kindergarten.

Not all of our young people are so fortunate. The schools are not permitted to speak of the raging hormones of their sexually maturing bodies or religion. Leaving them clueless in a "pile of shit" known as Media.

I found the following quote on Facebook this morning
"Before you speak, let your words pass through three gates.
At the first gate, ask yourself "Is it True?"
At the second gate, ask yourself "Is it Necessary?"
At the third gate "Is it Kind? " Sufi Saying

# ABOUT THE AUTHORS
## (Senior Scribes)

**Anna Chase.** I have always been an avid reader and an amateur writer and musician. I spent six years singing in an award winning a cappella chorus and another year in a gospel choir. I have also recently renewed my interest in playing piano. When I retired a few years ago, I joined a creative writing group and subsequently started a blog. I have experimented with many types of writing since joining the class, including poetry, short stories and essays. I am currently working on stories based on childhood memories about growing up in an Italian-American family.

**Anna Christian** is the author of five books, *The Newcomer*, latest in the Bobby & Sonny mystery series for preteens, 2013; *Daniel's Wife*, adult contemporary fiction, 2010; *The Big Table*, an illustrated children's book, 2008; *Mrs. Griffin is Missing and Other Stories*, Bobby & Sonny mystery series for preteens, 2005; and *Meet it, Greet it, and Defeat it! The Biography of Frances E. Williams, Actress/Activist*, 1999. A retired teacher, she has an M.A. in English from CSULA. In addition, she writes two blogs "Celebrating Life" on blogspot.com and a readers' blog on Goodreads.com. She facilitates the Creative Writing/Life Story class at the Moreno Valley Senior Center, and is a Heart & Soul Line Dance Instructor. Her websites are anachristian.com and francesplace.org.

**Stan Corella**, B.S. Degree in Human Services, Cal State Fullerton, Vocational Teaching Certificated Program, Cal State Long Beach. Vietnam Veteran, U. S. Army. Currently Retired and pursuing various interests which includes creative writing and current affairs.

**Ollie Eubany** I was born in New York, and met my husband, a Nigerian in 1958 in San Francisco. We later traveled to Nigeria where I lived for over 20 years. I wrote several articles for Nigerian Broadcasting Co. My articles were read on the radio. I am now writing my biography about my experience during the Nigerian/Biafran war.

In 1968, I was airlifted by the Red Cross from the war zone to Las Palmas and Madrid Spain. Two weeks later I was in New York. I returned to Nigeria in 1971 and wrote articles for Shell BP newsletter. I am now enjoying writing at the Moreno Valley Senior Center Life Story/Creative Writing class.

**Cathy Fortin-Jenkins** joined the Moreno Valley Senior Writers Group in 2009 for inspiration because she was compiling a book of family memories. She grew up in Central Pennsylvania, the youngest of ten children. So becoming the family historian fell upon her naturally. Her family history was well received by the family at their reunion in 2010. In addition to writing, Cathy also dabbles in oil painting and watercolor painting. She is the mother of three and has enjoyed living in Moreno Valley for the past twelve years.

**Nancy Graham** Retired accountant; B.S. degree in Political Science; Fiction Writing certificate, UCR; Working on three novels: German historical novel, WWII; biography of a WWII Dutch hero; past life mystery novel. I also breed Lhasa Apso puppies and buy/sell 1930-1950's dolls. I am also involved in helping abused, poor, and homeless children. I love my writing group and the WWII era!

**Anne Hendricks-Jones** grew up in Baltimore, Maryland, got her bachelor's degree at Wagner College, Staten Island, New York, and her masters at California State University at Dominguez Hills, California. After two years in the Peace Corp, she traveled and worked across the United States, as a medical technologist, and finally settled down in Moreno Valley, California. She retired in August of 2013 and with her husband of 32 years, has continued traveling the United States. Anne also enjoys all types of music, especially singing, reading, writing, and cooking (sometimes).

**Marcia Hill** is a retired Adult Education instructor. She taught the "Art of Dog and Cat Grooming" to people desiring to operate this type of business from 1984-2000. Marcia is a Certified Master Grooming registered with the National Dog Groomers Association of America. She is a past grooming judge for the International Judges Association. She has presented many seminars associated with pet care and business start-up for Barkleigh Productions in southern California and Pennsylvania. She has authored many articles pertaining to pet coat care. She has received numerous awards as an instructor, and the participation with the Groom and Kennel Expo shows.

**Jim Kraft** is 87 years old and is fooling no one. He is an old man who knows and feels it. His amazing accomplishment is his wonderful family. His earlier background included a BSEE degree from the University of Illinois (calculators were slide rulers), and a stateside stint in the U.S. Army Air Corp, World War II. His employment career was in the aircraft industry. He now works at the job he was always destined for, a volunteer in the Cancer Clinic at Riverside County Regional Medical Center. His outlook: We're here to have fun and make you happy.

**Pamela Kaiser Lowell**. I was born in Indianapolis, Indiana. In 1980 I moved to my current state of residence, California. My professional career consisted of government employment (city, county and state) and real estate. I have always been interested in writing. This time in my life is now affording me that opportunity which I am currently pursuing with the adventures of Molly and Zeus, short stories about my Labrador retrievers as well as other writings such as my poem, "Love Is Magic" included in this book.

**Rene Walter Madayski** was born on the estate of Mokre in Silesia Poland near Mikolow as the youngest of four siblings. This large estate was typical with acres, meadows and forests. His love of agriculture was already evident in his youth and would determine his lifelong ambitions. After his family was ethnically cleansed on orders of democratic mega-Hun Truman in cahoots with his British and

Bolshevist cronies, an order issued after the war in Europe had already ended, and engulfing almost 20 million eastern Europeans of various nationalities, he found himself now a survivor of this holocaust of ethnic cleansing, causing uncounted "trails and trains of tears" a penniless refugee in southern France on a farm, where he also learned viticulture, and later in Bavaria cheese making and dairy culture. The latter served as a toehold for his first job in the northern part of Illinois after his immigration. Later he worked daytime in factories in Chicago and studied at night. After earning his B.S., and a tour of duty with the U.S. Army in Alaska, he went to Michigan for his M.S. degree. The next 2 years saw him teaching science and riflery at a college preparatory school where he also served as a track coach. He then returned to the University of Michigan for his doctorate. He felt he owed this to his family. Every man in his family had a Ph.D., and every woman was married to one. Leaving Europe his father reminded him "We may be naked now, but we still have our pride". After graduation he accepted a position with a prominent West Coast university, from where he retired as professor emeritus. Reminiscing, he feels that he lived a successful and rewarding life despite its various ups and downs. He has been in over 60 countries, often on scientific endeavors, as symposium speaker or on germplasm collecting missions. Thus, he has friends worldwide. With diligence, hard work and perseverance he has achieved the American dream. His comment to his 3 children and every one who struggles to get ahead "Never give up. This country gives you the possibility to achieve what you desire, but you really have to assert yourself."

**Linda Moore** - I am now a retired schoolteacher. I retired last year. I was born and raised in Los Angeles. I grew up in Playa del Rey and the San Fernando Valley. I am married and presently live in Sunnymead Ranch. I have three grown children: Rachel, a social worker who lives in Oakland, Timmy who lives in Riverside, and Justin who lives in Davis and is a senior at U.C. Davis. I currently travel; I love to cruise. I do stitchery. I do pen and ink, acrylic painting, too. The last one I completed was "The Golden Girls." My passion when I retired was to publish my ex-students' stories "Where Are They Now?" It was completed and published on June 2014 in "Our Town News."

**Edith Nevins** - Mother of five adult children, eight grandchildren. A retired nurse of forty years. Received a B.A. in Communication. Community activist in several organizations in Cleveland, Ohio for over twenty-five years. A community activist in Moreno Valley Church as a Volunteer Tutor; secretary and member of a Christian book club; serves on the board of Quinn Community Outreach Corporation as Secretary and Health Educator for early detection of breast cancer. As a three-year proud member of the Life Story/Creative Writing Class, I have had many enjoyable weeks and months of writing, reading, and sharing ideas.

**Marge Ramsey** - I was born in Holbrook, Arizona to amazing parents. I moved to Hemet, California with my parents and two brothers at the age of four and remained there until graduating from high school and marrying my high school sweetheart, Tom. After three years of marriage, Tom and I planted our roots in "Sunnymead" in 1965 and have remained here ever since.

162

I had a professional career in accounting, but what I am really known for is my strength of character, and having a hand in raising four outstanding children; three natural daughters and one son adopted at the age of eight. My children will become my legacy.

I stared down lung cancer because dying didn't work for me, quit smoking after 34 years, and reprogrammed my life after the sudden death of my husband after 47 years of marriage. I have constant support and interaction with my family, and now believe I can take on any challenge life may bring my way.

**Phillip Sanchez** - I live in California; I am semi-retired staying active as a Realtor and still somewhat "in the game." I have been writing for most of my life but I have not really done anything to actually publish my works. This is my very first effort. I've written a lot of essays, poems and very short stories. I really do enjoy writing, fortunately, it is easy for me to get inspired and write something depending on my mood, where I am and what I am doing. Besides writing, I enjoy fishing, dancing and volunteering. I hope you enjoy these few writings.

**C.V. Schweitzer** was born on a farm south of Dodge City, Kansas in 1936. Graduated from St. Mary of the Plains College 1967. He traveled the world during his thirty years in the United States Air Force retiring with the rank of Chief Master Sergeant in 1989. He is a published author, "THE MAKING OF AN ANGEL" the adventures of a lost puppy and "THUMBS" the perils of hitchhiking in 2012 and "THE SHADOW OF THE RAINBOW" the aftermath of two shattered lives from the Viet Nam War in 2013. He is currently working on a number of short stories for further publication.

**Patsy Seo** - octogenarian living in Moreno Valley California. Born and raised in Parkersburg, West Virginia. I came from a God Fearing, God Loving Christian home and two solid mature loving parents. I was given a good start in life. Heading out with positive Goals. I knew what I wanted and planned to have it. I moved with my parents to Palm Springs, California. Most of my family have passed on to their reward. Happily I still have three beautiful grown and living daughters. Two by first husband and one borrowed from my second husband's family and never returned. I am retired, after more than 50 years as a licensed Clinical Laboratory Scientist. That is someone who works in a hospital laboratory. Retirement was Not my plan. I had planned to drop dead while still working. It has been more than two years now since I have had a job. Pretty positive that like it or not I have retired. God has watched over me. He has answered my prayers. Some with a firm no I understood immediately. Some I am so thankful I didn't succeed in getting. I am enjoying my retirement. I sing in the Moreno Valley Methodist Church Choir. I go to the Thursday Bible Study there, with our circle of friends, All women. I am studying Spanish and writing at the Senior Center. I would like to join their oil panting class as well; but have not yet mastered being two places at once. Yes, retirement is one of those things, I did not ask for but am happily enjoying. Last night I dreamed I was lost; for the first time in more than 70 years, I was not terrified at being lost. I realized after I woke this morning that home is where God is. God is everywhere.

**Mona Lisa Stallworth** - Writing has been my preferred form of communication for as long as I can remember. This, in spite of the fact, that none of my English teachers or professors ever found my writing to be noteworthy. But, thank God, for Moreno Valley Senior Creative Writing class I joined last year. Here, among my fellow Senior Scribes, I found individuals that loved, understood and appreciated my writings. For me there is nothing more rewarding than to be able to share my hopes, dreams, disappointments, wisdom and words of encouragement and inspiration with others through my written words. I am a writer.

**Al Turnbull**, age 87 - since joining the Creative Writing Class in 2009 has contributed 95 short stories, 56 non-fiction pieces along with numerous poems. He is a retired school psychologist. His interests include family, travel, and playing the organ.

www.ingramcontent.com/pod-product-compliance
Lightning Source LLC
Chambersburg PA
CBHW051828170626
46807CB00003B/1084